A WILL
AND A WAY

A WILL
AND A WAY

A woman with roots in one century and wings in another encourages all women to discover their ability to shape the future.

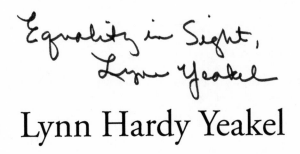

Equality in Sight,
Lynn Yeakel

Lynn Hardy Yeakel

Library of Congress Control Number:		2010906961
ISBN:	Hardcover	978-1-4535-0123-8
	Softcover	978-1-4535-0122-1
	Ebook	978-1-4535-0124-5

This book was printed in the United States of America.

To order additional copies of this book, contact:
Xlibris Corporation
1-888-795-4274
www.Xlibris.com
Orders@Xlibris.com
75857

CONTENTS

Dedication

Courtney, Martín, Max, Chloe, and Joaquin Arias
Paul, Pilar, Mae, Wesley, and Russell Yeakel

Introduction

When I was running for the U.S. Senate in 1992, a reporter asked me, "Are you running like a woman?" I paused, and then replied, "I didn't know I had a choice."

Can you imagine asking a man such a question? It was one of many puzzling issues I had to deal with in what the national media dubbed "The Year of the Woman in Politics." It was a year when many of us stepped forward to try and change an institution that so profoundly affects all of our lives—yet does not adequately represent us.

That question, substituting the word "writing" for "running," might well be asked in relation to this book, and my answer would be the same. I am writing from the perspective of a woman who came of age in the second half of the twentieth century and was an active participant in the pivotal social movements that changed women's lives and shaped women's futures.

In the self-help section of any bookstore it doesn't take long to locate numerous similar recommendations for how to have a successful life. They say "be yourself." That's probably good advice. You ought to be pretty good at being you. No one is more qualified for the job.

That's what I thought when I was growing up. I never wanted to be the typical daughter, the sidekick wife, the *Good Housekeeping* homemaker of the year. My life has had its limited moments of sharing recipes, sewing on buttons, and making crab dip. Some women are wonderful cooks and I admire them. I'm just not one of them. I've lived a relatively independent life, despite some seemingly traditional lifestyle choices, and I've been fortunate to have had more advantages than many others.

Beyond caring for and enjoying the family I love, I learned early that it was part of my DNA to speak up and stand up for the rights of women, who for so many centuries have lived lives as second-class citizens, often denied opportunities to discover their human potential.

Making the case for women's equality has been accompanied by controversy and confrontation—as well as applause and appreciation. "Change" usually brings both. When I put myself and my views out there, I anticipated some of the criticism and ridicule that invariably fall upon those who take public positions on key issues. But I gritted my teeth and tried to separate myself from the risk-averse behavior I've seen too often in women. I did not want to be intimidated by the warning, "If you can't stand the heat, get back in the kitchen."

Both the heat and the harmony I experienced during an extraordinary time for American women fill the pages of these essays, which speak about what's been accomplished and what's unfinished on the agenda of equality. What's done we can celebrate. What's unfinished can be found in the questions this collection poses. What connects each essay, each question, is a common theme of optimism and encouragement for all women to say, "I will do what I can to make the opportunity to 'be yourself' a reality, not a dream."

I have used the pronoun "we" in the essay titles to refer to women, especially women of my generation. But I believe these are messages for women of all generations, and for men too. They are lessons learned, and they are intended to urge all of us to live our lives to the fullest and to try and tackle tough challenges, even if we sometimes come up short. I have done both. The important point is to put our fears aside and attempt to fix what's not right. In doing so, we will make life better for all.

—Lynn Hardy Yeakel

Acknowledgments

It is customary on this page to thank all the people who had something to do with making this publication possible. I won't do that. All who helped me know who you are and how grateful I am for what you did. My gratitude can best be conveyed by continuing the work I feel is so valuable. I will do that. You can count on it.

CHAPTER 1

As We Reach for the Peaks,
Can We Cope with the Valleys?

Some Americans are bilingual. They speak
English and they speak silence. I'm not good at
silence, particularly when I hear women belittled
or women's concerns marginalized. My instinct
is to speak up and take action if necessary,
knowing that it may lead to either the elation
of spectacular achievement or the isolation of
crushing disappointment. When the cause is lost,
I liken it to being abandoned on an island. Women
are all too familiar with that feeling.

The way the city planners laid out Philadelphia, the dominant
thoroughfare is Broad Street. It runs for 12 straight-as-a-string miles, north
to the suburbs, south to the Navy Yard and busy Sports Complex.

City Hall is the centerpiece, interrupting block-after-block of buildings
devoted to commerce and culture. One stretch is even called Avenue of the
Arts, reflecting a concentration of performing arts venues.

It is a street of parades for championship sports teams that don't win
often enough for sports-hungry fans, but when victory comes, Broad Street
becomes a superhighway for celebrations.

It can also be a boulevard of broken dreams.

The Hilton Hotel on Broad Street has changed names since November
1992 but has always been a popular location in Philadelphia. The hotel's
ballroom was named for famous Philadelphia Orchestra conductor Eugene
Ormandy. It was an ideal hall for large gatherings, like election night
parties—those made-for-television events featuring balloons, bands, and
adult beverages, all held together by high hopes and whatever cash remained
after a tough campaign.

And my campaign team knew how to stage a victory party. We had done that successfully just six months earlier when I won the Democratic Primary in my run for the United States Senate. It had been a joyous April evening, capping a stunning—and surprising—triumph for a candidate who only two months earlier had polled a lowly one percent name recognition in Pennsylvania.

The *Philadelphia Inquirer* covered the upset of sitting Lieutenant Governor Mark Singel by writing, "The pundits, the operatives, the reporters, the political insiders, the hangers-on all were amazed."

The champagne tasted especially good on that last Tuesday in April. We made a note to order the same vintage for election night in November.

The decision to seek the U.S. Senate seat held by incumbent Arlen Specter had been one of those "Edgar Guest" moments in my life. When I was a child growing up in Virginia, my father loved to quote an Edgar Guest homily. He did some editing, changing the pronoun to fit my gender.

Somebody said it couldn't be done
But she, with a chuckle, replied
That maybe it couldn't but she would be one
Who wouldn't say so 'til she tried.

My commitment to a life of service and advocacy for women did not really originate with me. It was a product of a school I attended early and often. It was the "school of the possible," open seven days a week, with a faculty of one—my father.

The curriculum was not complicated. Be of value. Make good decisions. Do your best. Make things better. And, above all, *never quit!*

What I had tried, for all the right reasons, in the 1992 Year of the Woman, was to go against the political odds. Having never run for office, I knew that this would be a high hill to climb, but I also knew it was what needed to be done to express the anger that I and so many other women were feeling. We were angry over the abusive treatment Anita Hill had received from the men of the U.S. Senate Judiciary Committee, who had unrelentingly grilled her during her sexual harassment testimony against Supreme Court nominee Clarence Thomas.

In particular, I felt that the senior senator from my home state of Pennsylvania, Arlen Specter, had shown disrespect for her in the militant way he conducted his questioning. He challenged her truthfulness and asked demeaning questions. He and the thirteen other white men on the

Judiciary Committee were verbally attacking an African American woman, a distinguished law professor. They humiliated her, and a senator from my state was the ringleader in this abuse.

The television spectacle reminded me of the haunting images of so many newspaper photographs I had seen through the years of white males in positions of power making decisions about women—without a single woman in the room. I felt strongly that a woman needed to challenge Arlen Specter.

Other women nationwide were seeking Senate seats. Among them were Dianne Feinstein and Barbara Boxer in California, Carol Moseley Braun in Illinois, and Patty Murray in Washington. I had to try. No other woman in Pennsylvania was stepping forward.

What followed was an upset primary win in April, subsequent statewide, national and even international media attention I had not anticipated, and six months of hardball political campaign reality, all leading to that night in November 1992. It was a race that, according to national media, was "too close to call." So there I was with my family in my hotel suite at the Hilton on Broad Street surrounded by supporters, waiting for the election results that would either send me off to Washington or make me a footnote in the long history of American politics. Hundreds, including most of my longtime friends, had gathered in the ballroom downstairs. Their excitement built as early returns showed that I was ahead. A television report even teased us with a hint that Specter was preparing to concede.

When my campaign staff handed me gracious remarks for an acceptance speech, I also asked them to prepare a concession statement. I've always believed in being prepared in case things don't turn out the way I hope.

No one would work on the concession option, so I finally closeted myself in the suite's bedroom and wrote down some remarks of my own. It was a lonely exercise, but I knew the world would be watching—literally—and I was not at all certain of the outcome.

Most women have plenty of experience with disappointment. Whether it's being turned down for a job we know we can do, being excluded from a club or a board room, or being ignored in a meeting when one of us makes a good suggestion that a man subsequently gets credit for, most of us do not take success for granted. We work hard for the best but also have experience in coping with the worst.

Certainly that's the way things were when I graduated from college in 1963 and went to New York to look for a job. The ubiquitous question "can you type?" was my first dose of reality about women's options being different from men's. And then there were the parental and societal expectations about marriage. At that time, the optimal accomplishment for a woman in her twenties was to find a husband.

The Way We Were is the title of one of my favorite movies, but in terms of expectations and opportunities for women in the second half of the twentieth century, that phrase was unacceptable to me. I just couldn't accept the way things were.

In 1987, the City of Philadelphia hosted the celebration of the bicentennial of the United States Constitution.

The key event of the year was a ceremony in front of Independence Hall. The flags were unfurled. The marching bands stepped off with precision. Public officials blossomed in staggering numbers. President Ronald Reagan showed up for this historic occasion.

I was there also, as a member of the We the People 200 Advisory Committee, sitting in the crowd, proud to be in attendance but thoroughly puzzled by what I was seeing.

There were over one hundred people on the stage, a number that challenged the structural integrity of the temporary platform. Each person was deftly competing for a positioning edge to become politically more visible.

Over one hundred men—and *not one woman*!

I glanced quickly at my pocket-sized edition of the Constitution. Sure enough, the document began with "We the people . . ." written by men, being celebrated two hundred years later, still by men only.

I took a photograph that day of all those men on the stage and had the picture enlarged. It hung in my office and the caption I put on it was, "What's wrong with this picture?"

Five years later I was trying to change that by running for the U.S. Senate.

We ran a clean campaign, worked hard, raised $5 million from fifty-two thousand people all over America. And on November 3, 1992, although 2.2 million Pennsylvanians cast their votes for me, it was not quite enough.

Late-night returns from western Pennsylvania, where the National Rifle Association was especially strong and vigorously opposed to my position on gun control, showed Specter gradually overtaking my early lead. The final margin was a heartbreaker. But the result was irreversible. Arlen Specter was going back to Washington after winning 49 percent of the vote to my 47 percent—with the balance going to a third party candidate.

Almost immediately I could sense being alone on the island, and there was a dreaded concession speech to deliver.

The mood change was instant, and my hotel suite emptied quickly. There was a dazed look on the faces of my supporters who had worked so hard.

It had been much easier to give the victory talk in April. Nothing in my life had prepared me for the disappointment I was experiencing. Even as I spoke the obligatory words of congratulations to Senator Specter over the phone and took the stage to deliver my farewell remarks to a saddened crowd downstairs, I felt an undertow of emotion pulling the sand from beneath my feet.

People said all the right things. We had fought the good fight. We had clearly communicated that women were no longer going to tolerate the kind of treatment Anita Hill had undergone. We had proved that women can mobilize in massive numbers and organize an effective political campaign.

There was to be no gold medal, although in later years I would see that winning the silver had some enduring value.

But not that night. The transition from high anticipation to sudden sadness was abrupt. People were taking down the decorations. My family was heading home. The media representatives who had followed my every moment for six months were packing their gear. Grown men and women with tears in their eyes fumbled for their parking garage tickets.

I tried the champagne. Same as April, but it tasted flat this time.

I went back to my room feeling very much alone.

I had no plans. After all, I had given up my job, all my volunteer activities, and even my precious independence to run. Having been driven around for months for the sake of security, I didn't even have a "getaway" car readily available. And, as I found out the next day, my campaign was a half million dollars in debt. There were no rescue ships on the horizon and no helicopters waiting to lift me out of my isolation. If I was going to get off the island, it would be the same as it has always been for women. I was going to have to figure it out for myself.

I tried to remember what someone had told me—that there was never a night so dark that it could blot out the arrival of a new day. I reminded myself that it had been a year of splendid achievement and roller-coaster disillusionment. To be the kind of woman I wanted to be, I had to handle both extremes.

Maybe revisiting my roots would help. It had worked for others.

CHAPTER 2

How Do We Measure the Impact of "Family?"

I believe in plunging into the deep end of life's pool, unafraid to pursue worthwhile goals and unwilling to retreat just because a challenge has not yet been overcome or because an army of critics is poised to second-guess my actions. Doing this can put a woman in a wilderness of her own creation. Later in life, looking for where to place the blame or record the credit, "family" becomes a convenient and sometimes accurate focal point.

Once I was asked by an interviewer who it was that had the most influence on my life.

I said, "My father and my mother."

"Too easy," said the interviewer. "Everybody says their heroes are their moms and dads. Think about it some more and we'll talk again."

I took the suggestion and thought about that question a lot. Probably for sixty years. I still have the same answer. I've met presidents, worked with chief executives of Fortune 500 firms, met and mingled with hundreds of achievers in education and the arts.

It still goes back to Porter Hardy Jr. and Lynn Moore Hardy.

My father, because he taught me to expect the best from myself and others, and that there is no limit to what you can achieve if you never permit yourself to be outworked.

My mother, because she taught me to be respectful of others, not to complain, and that wherever I decided to go, to always remember where I came from.

From my dad I learned to be direct, independent and determined (some might say stubborn). Be self-reliant, he urged me. Have a commitment to service and never compromise your integrity. Be unafraid of big challenges. Don't give up on something just because it's difficult.

At the core of my father's life and beliefs was his faith. The message, "be a good Christian," was never clearly defined, but I was expected to know what it meant and to demonstrate those values in the life I led.

My mother was a "Southern Lady" in the best sense of that phrase. Under her 1930 graduation photo in the Agnes Scott College yearbook, she was described as "our tall and dignified Lynn." She maintained her dignity through years of adversity that included the deaths of my brother and father, her long struggles with Parkinson's disease and blindness, and the indignities of old age that led to her total dependence on others in the years leading to her death at age ninety-seven.

She rarely expressed personal pain, and I never saw her cry, even after my brother was killed at age forty-three in a tragic pedestrian auto accident or when my father died after fifty-five years of marriage. When I asked her about her grief, she said, "I grew up in Tennessee. We don't cry in Tennessee."

From her I learned social graces—there was always an etiquette book nearby—a love of fine clothes and treasures and loyalty and perseverance. She had been a schoolteacher and school principal in rural East Tennessee before she married my father, and one of the lessons she taught with her lifestyle is that the basic structure of human government is the family.

I've visited that theory often in life. It stands up pretty well. A family is a democracy. It debates, legislates, enforces, budgets, administers—often more efficiently than an elected government.

When you're a teenage girl you are convinced that in family government too much power is concentrated in the executive branch. Parents are the ones who make rules, set curfews and control the car.

When a woman becomes a mother and therefore feels entitled to the family power that she imagined went with the office, she often discovers that isn't true. Children, encouraged to "be themselves," shock us when they do just that. It's called rebellion.

Every woman develops a value system, a catalog of principles that are important to her. Our startup kit is inherited from our family of origin. We may edit as we go along, deleting traits we feel are obsolete, and adding others adopted from the lives of people whose characteristics capture our admiration.

Most of us have had role models and though not all women role models have marquee names, their messages are indelible if we examine what their lives had to say.

If it's courage you admire, find out more about Olympic gold medalist Wilma Rudolph who, because of a series of childhood illnesses, could not walk until she was eight. For therapy, she began to run and did so better than most despite continuing bouts with bad health. In 1960, in Rome, before a world audience, she became the first American woman to win three gold medals.

Her fluid running style electrified fans and would lead her to fame that could not have been forecast for this shut-in girl from Clarksville, Tennessee. Just as admirable as her athleticism was her attitude. She was a woman of poise, dignity, humility—all those things my mother, the schoolteacher, told me would one day be important to me.

If it's perseverance you're seeking, study Sarah Stevenson who in the sixty-eight years she lived, mostly in the nineteenth century, defied the obstacles and objections to women becoming physicians and practiced medicine with such brilliance that she became the first woman to be welcomed as a member of the American Medical Association at its convention in Philadelphia in America's centennial year of 1876.

Or if responsibility fascinates you, learn all you can about Julia Parker, a telephone operator in the early part of the twentieth century who became enraged at the low pay and poor working conditions of her colleagues and reached at the age of twenty-two for responsibility in organizing and leading labor unions. She would become an international labor leader, a key figure in the campaigns of four-term President Franklin D. Roosevelt, and in the meantime would raise two girls and outlive her husband by twelve years.

In the words of Eleanor Roosevelt: "Remember always that you not only have the right to be an individual, you have an obligation to be one."

Individuality. That's what my father demonstrated to me. It wasn't so much what he said. It was how he lived his life.

Both my parents' families have a long history in America, dating back to the seventeenth century. The Hardys came from England and landed in Yorktown, Virginia, a state they never left. There was a Hardy in the first Continental Congress, and seventy-five years later another one, my great-grandfather, in the War Between The States.

My mother's maternal ancestors, the Courtneys and McFarlanes, came from Scotland through Pittsburgh, Pennsylvania, and eventually settled in Tennessee.

The long family legacies were a source of pride and there was the ever-present message that I was expected to uphold the families' good names. When I got into trouble as a teenager, I was sternly reminded of that obligation.

My father was the son of a Methodist minister. The Methodist Church moved its ministers every two years, so the six Hardy children and their parents lived in parsonages all over Virginia during my grandfather's forty-six-year ministry.

For my father, education was wherever he was, including at home in the early years. He was a bright student who finished high school at age sixteen and graduated from Randolph-Macon College in three years, at age nineteen.

He was admitted to Harvard's Business Administration Graduate School, a splendid experience in education and a sobering one in economics, for it took him seven years to pay off the money he borrowed for his one-year Ivy League adventure.

The woman he would meet and marry, Lynn Moore, was the second of five girls. Their father, R. Locke Moore, owned a Dodge-Plymouth dealership in the small town of Morristown, Tennessee, where he survived the Great Depression with cash payments for cars from moonshine entrepreneurs in the surrounding mountains. When I was born, I was named for my mother, Lynn Moore Hardy, and there was little doubt about what my brother would be called. He became Porter Hardy III, and years later his son would bring fourth and fifth generation continuity to the name.

My mother was what we now call a stay-at-home mom. Although that role never appealed to me for very long stretches of time, I have total appreciation for the skills and versatility required to manage a household. During my father's political career, my mother actually faced the additional challenge of maintaining a second home.

I have always found it infuriating when women who enter the workplace after managing households and raising families are turned down for jobs because they "lack experience." If employers could identify the marketable skills these women have accumulated in handling budgets, juggling schedules, settling personnel disputes, making decisions, they would find people who know the value of hard work.

My mother provided the grounding and support for our family, enabling the promising Virginia farmer and businessman to become a U.S. Congressman. When he did, she stayed in the background—and I grew up wondering why she didn't want more, knowing that I would.

It was the middle of the twentieth century and most married women—if they didn't need the income—were in the traditional role of homemaker while their husbands were "winning bread." My mother and father each had four sisters, and all but one, who had married young, had a college degree. Without exception, they were strong, intelligent women who could have avoided being dependent financially. The only one who worked outside the home was my father's unmarried sister, a high school teacher, and I remember associating her with the "Old Maid" in the card game that I came to realize was terribly demeaning to women. Everyone felt sorry for Frances Hardy because she never landed a husband and had to support herself, with regular financial assistance from her brother, my father, who having grown up poor became the generous provider for all his family members who needed help.

As these realities made their way into my consciousness—along with my father's constant advice about the importance of economic independence—I began to think about a career. During high school I dreamed of becoming a psychiatrist because I was fascinated with how the mind works, until I learned how many years of medical school, on top of college, were required to attain that degree. The first priority, after all, was to find a husband.

For women the message of individuality was not an easy one to absorb. Going it alone sounded charismatic, but for women it was against the wind.

It doesn't take many steps into adulthood to recognize that the world is a place for couples. So many events are "couple things." Single women often are not included on invitation lists and many feel uncomfortable going alone to a social event.

That isn't right, but it's real, and it takes a strong woman to deal with that. Some can carry it off. Others find it easier just to stay home. Most of us overcome it by finding a partner.

I was married at twenty-three, at the time almost old age for a bride. Paul Yeakel was a charming, attractive graduate of the University of Pennsylvania's Wharton School who would become a successful investment banking executive. I was a year out of Randolph-Macon Woman's College, working in New York City. We met in New York and were married six months later.

Paul knew from the beginning that I valued my identity. I had rebelled against being known as "Porter Hardy's daughter." I rejected the possessive idea of being introduced as "Paul Yeakel's wife." I had a name and wanted to be known by it, although I never seriously considered keeping my family name when we married.

That pride in one's own identity was a gift from my father. He provided other gifts, like demonstrating how each positive step of one's life can set the stage for transition to the next opportunity.

Serving eleven terms in the U.S. Congress was never on his "to do" list, but it happened because it was the next natural step in his lifetime agenda of service. He had taken up farming in order to provide a home for his aging parents when his father retired from the ministry.

He became a leader among farmers in Virginia and helped them found the Virginia Farm Bureau. His interest there led him to travel to Washington in the 1930s to meet with the new Secretary of Agriculture so he could learn firsthand about the new federal Agricultural Adjustment Act. He became an expert on that legislation and a frequent speaker to farmers' groups.

A decade later, his friends convinced him that he could be of more help to his community as an advocate inside Congress. In 1944, he narrowly lost a race for the U.S. House of Representatives. Two years later, he ran again and won. His campaign budget: $1,400.

When he was sworn in as a freshman congressman in 1947, others in that class included a young man from Massachusetts, John Fitzgerald Kennedy. The two became close friends.

Also in that group of newcomers was a man from California named Richard Nixon. My father never warmed up to Nixon. Neither did that Irishman from Massachusetts.

After twenty-two years of distinguished service, my father retired from Congress, saying "*Too many members stay around too long. That's not what the founding fathers intended.*"

Praise from his colleagues and the media included words like "honorable" and "gentleman" and "patriot." Most of all he left a legacy of hard work, and years later he told me that what he liked most about his years in Congress was his ability to help people. It was a message not lost on me.

Parents are in the unique position to push you out of the nest while at the same time trying to protect you from the evils of the very world they are encouraging you to encounter.

This was particularly true for girls. Boys were urged to compete. Girls were taught to compromise. Boys were given big goals. Girls were told to play it safe. As far back as high school I was asking, "Why?"

During my 1992 campaign for the U.S. Senate, *Philadelphia* magazine published a feature story about me entitled "The Lady or the Tiger?" I believe the answer to that question is "Yes, both." I inherited my father's adventurous character, desire to serve, and feisty personality. But I also absorbed my mother's sense of social propriety, good manners, and consideration of other people. That combination of traits would sometimes come into conflict as I pursued my goals in the world of politics.

CHAPTER 3

If the Elevator to Independence Is Out of Order, Are We Willing to Take the Stairs?

> Most progress for women has depended on a certain number of us being unreasonable. When there is an imbalance in the scales of justice, it takes people who are unafraid to break the rules they believe are unfair. The teenage years are ripe for challenging the behavioral code. That's when girls stop telling their parents where they've been, what they've been doing and who with. As a mother, you dread the loss of control. As the person growing up, you can't wait to stretch the standards.

I identify with Anne Henrietta Martin.

Hers is not a household name, but if you are a student of women's history, you know that she was the first woman to run for a seat in the United States Senate.

She did that in Nevada in 1918 when women didn't have the vote, and again in 1920 when they did. Told that "the rules prohibit you from running," Anne Martin responded, "And whose rules are those?"

"Equality for women is a passion with me," she said and backed up her belief with vigorous support of the campaign for the right to vote, even to the point of being arrested for picketing the White House in 1918.

I know how she felt. I sometimes substitute the word "justice" for "equality," but the idea is the same as Martin's. The identity goes even deeper.

Her motivation, not unlike mine, to use the fundamentals learned in the family classroom and undertake a life devoted to overcoming barriers facing women came from her father, who was a successful Reno businessman. He had encouraged her to become educated and introduced her to populist ideas that jump-started her social conscience.

Her mother, not unlike mine, would have preferred to see Anne Martin learn to sew and grow to be a proper wife, but quietly cheered on her daughter's unquenchable thirst to achieve change.

The death of her father in 1901, when she was twenty-six, created some family turbulence during the settling of his estate. Anne Martin spoke up in protest of the way her father's business interests had been mismanaged by his partners. Her four brothers disagreed. In the end, her mother rejected her advice and followed the wishes of her brothers.

"This suddenly made a feminist of me," she said. "I found I stood alone in my family against a man-controlled world."

When her portion of the inheritance was received, she used most of it to travel to Europe and that proved to be the turning point of her life. It was there that she joined and became a leader among suffragists.

My reasons for going to Europe during my junior year in college were not so dramatic, but they did involve a need for freedom. It's not easy to explain, even now, why I wanted to get away from a family that loved me dearly, a college that treated me kindly, a circle of friends who cared about me genuinely.

Up until then I had never really made a major decision of my own. When I did, it was a decision to study abroad for a year.

Leading up to that moment, most of my life choices had been made for me and the expectations laid out for me to follow. Mostly by my father.

He controlled the finances, establishing a bank account for me for which I had no responsibility except to write checks for small amounts as needed. While that may sound enviable in some ways, what I never considered at the time was that the monthly bank statements were going to my parents. They were aware of every check I wrote. Talk about control!

On behavior, my parents tried to call most of the shots. Church and family had taught me that alcohol and sex were bad, and movies and card games on Sunday were forbidden. I became determined to find out about all those things earlier than I should have.

My junior year in France meant a release from control. The urge for liberation had been building for a long time. I had been in girls-only educational surroundings most of my life. Growing up as the daughter of a congressman had its privileges—attending the same school as President Dwight Eisenhower's grandchildren and being excused from class so I could join my father in a visit with Queen Elizabeth are two examples. But it also had its downside—the constant threat of unwanted attention and bad publicity because of his public life.

It was what I now recognize was a mixed message—a near-fantasy set of experiences that would help me understand in later years what power can achieve in a positive way, and at the same time it was a protective and oppressive wall around me, preventing me from sampling reality.

My inclination to push against the rules took on real form in those years on the Randolph-Macon Woman's College campus in Lynchburg, Virginia.

As much as I respected the school and its traditions, if I didn't think a rule was fair, I'd ignore it. It wasn't just to challenge authority for the sport of it, but to question regulations that didn't seem to be enriched in common sense.

There was a "no-drinking-within-25-miles-of-the-campus" rule which seemed crazy to me, and to others. If you wanted a drink, as most college-age people did, you had to go far enough away so that the drive back could be dangerous if the driver had too much to drink.

Curfews didn't make much sense to me, or the rule about "staying only at approved houses" when visiting campuses where our dates were.

Many of the women accepted such rules. I objected to what I felt was irrational or unfair. It occurred to me at some point that my joy in going to France may well have been shared by the faculty and staff at Randolph-Macon watching me go.

What my time in Europe, particularly in Paris, did for me was to help me discover I could take care of myself. I was no longer sheltered from decision-making. Until I arrived there, I had studied. While in Europe, I learned. There is a difference.

My choices were my own. My mistakes belonged to me. My wins in and out of the classroom, my excesses and occasional regrets—they were of my own doing. And I loved it. It was really the first time I had moved from the theory of independence to the practice of it.

Any structure that subjects women to a secondary status or function annoyed me then—and outrages me now.

I'm not sure when I first began to resent the term "auxiliaries."

I remember hearing that word applied to women's groups in churches or to men-only boards of directors where the women raised the money and the men decided how to spend it. To me a "Ladies Auxiliary" was there as a support arm and an afterthought of something men already controlled.

The dictionary defines "auxiliary" as "supplementing . . . supporting . . . assisting . . . giving help to." That's not a role I care for. I favor shared responsibility. Women ought to be in the room when the plans are formulated, the decisions are made, the resources allocated.

The very term "auxiliary" implies that women in those circumstances are acting in a subordinate capacity.

In the 1970s, when I was involved in establishing Women's Way, the first fundraising federation of agencies run by and for women, one of our initial moves was to create a "men's auxiliary" to help with our fundraising campaign. Women's Way was an independent organization, created and managed by women to provide ongoing financial support to important services for women and families, and to provide a way for people to give to those programs. The men's auxiliary was a tongue-in-cheek support arm that generated some fun publicity.

Independence is the pivotal quality in achieving individual rights. Without it, we are second-class citizens, incapable of defining our destiny, and all the more vulnerable to a future dictated by others.

That decision I made in college to go to Europe was not motivated by academic zeal. Education was not at the top of my list. "Getting away" was.

Such a feeling at the time, the early '60s, illustrates the push/pull conflict going on in my life. Comfort was pulling me to stay where I was in familiar surroundings. Curiosity was pushing me to go to where I hadn't been, in hopes that at the end of the rainbow, the prize would be independence.

The conflict was on multiple levels, and fascinating to me. It goes on to this day.

At that time, I wanted to get away from the all-women atmosphere of my educational experience, even though I believe that single-sex education helps foster leadership qualities and self-confidence in women, qualities that for some may be submerged on a coed campus.

I wanted to get away from parents who so closely governed my life, even though my sense of having outgrown them was incorrect, and I knew even then that I would cling for a lifetime to the value system they had given me.

I wanted to get away from the imagined requirements of religious and other rules imposed on me, which I believed were unnecessary and unfair, even though later I would embrace my faith and other moral principles that would be sustaining.

The road to independence is not without potholes, but when you're young, the exhilaration of freedom is intoxicating.

I loved the liberty that came with my year abroad—the parties, the stay-up-late, do-what-you-want freedom of making my own decisions.

For the first time, I was challenged by the real competition of other people's ideas. I enjoyed engaging in discussions with people who disagreed with me. I found out something I should have already known about myself. Heated arguments don't bother me. Losing them does. My participation in the college debate team confirmed this.

I was not very interested in athletics when I was growing up. I could swim and play tennis, but I discovered early that boys generally have a physical edge over girls in competitive sports.

So I competed in games where I could consistently win. One of those was chess. Another was bridge. Both are brain games in which it doesn't matter how tall you are or how fast you run. Beating boys or men in a chess game or bridge game was a victory for strategic thinking where I felt I had a home field advantage.

Finding out what we're good at is an essential element in women's quest to achieve equal footing. Thousands of years of organized religion and English law combined to relegate women to the role of producing boys who would grow up to be men of leadership, and producing girls who would grow up to produce more boys to make our decisions for us.

The U.S. Constitution did not specify that women were to be second-class citizens, but rather implied we were not citizens at all. That every one of the first forty-four presidents was male seems more than a trend, more than a coincidence.

In most parts of our civilization, men had been carefully taught to make the big decisions, and women had been equally disciplined to obey them. The second half of the twentieth century seemed like a good time to change that.

CHAPTER 4

Will Justice Come If We Wait Long Enough?

When your life is carefully choreographed by the expectations of others, there is not much room for flexibility. The idea that a woman might want to chart a course of her own was uncomfortable to a society convinced it knew what was best for the "weaker sex." The time was coming when a woman's place would be wherever she wanted it to be, but first we had to learn the lessons of the '50s and '60s—that in order to achieve civil rights, a nation has to correct uncivil wrongs.

I danced with President John F. Kennedy.

The location was 1600 Pennsylvania Avenue in Washington D.C. The occasion was the annual Congressional Ball held at the White House.

It was January of 1963. My father was entering his seventeenth year as a congressman from Virginia. I was in my senior year of college and was beginning to wonder what I wanted to do after graduation.

My date that night at the White House was my father. My mother had unselfishly stayed home so that I might be part of an evening that would predictably be among life's most treasured moments. You never know when you're going to make a memory, but this night I fully expected to be special.

My long red strapless gown was just right. I felt grown-up and confident.

I can't remember all the details of that evening, but I'll never forget one. I was asked to dance by John F. Kennedy, my father's old friend from their earliest days in the House of Representatives together who was now president of the United States. Two years earlier, on a cold January morning, I had sat with my parents at the foot of the Capitol steps for President Kennedy's inauguration. His charm, charisma, and promise of new, exciting leadership had lifted the spirits of so many Americans and the hopes of many people around the world, and now his attention was focused solely on me.

I've been asked, "Was he a good dancer?" That I don't recall, but I do have a vivid mental picture of an incredibly handsome man.

On a night that was already unreal, something else happened.

At one point, while my father and I were talking with a group of people, the cigarette case I was holding slipped out of my hand and the cigarettes scattered on the ballroom floor. Smoking for a young college girl was considered acceptable in those days as a rite of passage to adulthood, although my parents disapproved.

Before I could pick up the cigarettes, a rather distinguished Southern gentleman beat me to it. His name was Lyndon Baines Johnson, and he was vice president of the United States. He was a charmer of a different sort.

John Kennedy, whom my father continued to call Jack when he was president, a serious breach of protocol as my mother constantly reminded him, was a hero of mine. It was his campaign in 1960 that ignited my first real political activity. I helped found a Young Democrats chapter on my college campus that year.

When my father had run for office it seemed more like a job, something he did for a living. Maybe I was too close at the time to understand how dedicated he was to public service and to sense how much of that commitment was working its way into my community service bloodstream.

How could the year of 1963 that started out so gloriously end so tragically?

President Kennedy was assassinated in Dallas, Lyndon Johnson became the president, and the clouds of a war in a faraway place called Vietnam were beginning to gather.

Before the decade was out, that war would engulf America and in many ways divide us as a nation. Antiwar protests, two more crushing assassinations—of Civil Rights leader Martin Luther King Jr. and Robert Kennedy—and unrest on college campuses as well as in the streets of our cities, would make the '60s competitive with the most turbulent times in American history.

Civil Rights had finally surfaced in the midfifties and the issue did so in a succession of marches and violent confrontations as the plight of African American people fought for a beachhead on the nation's conscience. The year I was a freshman in college, two women in the senior class participated in a sit-in at a lunch counter in Lynchburg and spent a month in jail. Controversy was everywhere.

The struggle was pushed into the national spotlight by the courageous act of Rosa Parks challenging her right to sit on a bus, and the high profile marches led by the Rev. Dr. Martin Luther King Jr. What amplified those events was the emergence of television as an every night, in-your-face source of information.

As television newsgathering became more sophisticated and networks found that it was a lucrative means of building audiences and revenues, coverage began to have direct impact on the progress of civil rights.

Public opinion is a splendid moving force once it is motivated in a productive direction. Civil Rights in the 1960s was an idea that was long overdue. Communications made it happen. Since Martin Luther King Jr.'s "I have a dream" speech in Washington was not confined to a single audience at a single time, it became a turning point in history.

The arousal of public interest in women's rights had no such seminal event during the '60s. A look at history would have told us that civil rights and women's rights were linked by the same theme—a denial of fundamental freedom.

A century earlier, two African American women who were legends in the fight against slavery had already made the connection.

In 1867 Sojourner Truth said, "If colored men get their rights and women don't, men will be masters over women and it will be just as bad as before."

In 1869 Harriet Tubman said, "There was one or two things I as a woman had a right to, liberty or death. If I could not have one, I would have the other, for no man should take me alive."

With so much change going on in 1963, I was ready to finish my college experience and move on to a more active life. I began to make plans to join a friend who was living in New York City.

There was an assumption at that time that for a woman, going into a career to see what you could accomplish would be just a brief interlude as well as an indication that you had not yet identified a prospective husband by graduation day.

The stampede for women to marry early might have been slowed if we had paused to read George Bernard Shaw's definition of marriage. He wrote: "When two people are under the influence of the most violent, most insane, most delusive, and most transient of passions, they are required to swear that they will remain in that excited, abnormal, and exhausting condition continuously until death do them part."

Women had more to offer than being homemakers, and in the 1960s, we were beginning to get some indications that new doors for us, if not wide open, were at least ajar. The introduction of the birth control pill, enabling us to control our reproductive lives, played the major role in this realization.

Did the Civil Rights struggle accelerate the pace of Women's Rights?

It certainly helped. The national attention clearly illustrated that America had a lot of catching up to do on race relations. Women took the cue and began to communicate their grievances.

An America smart enough to land Neil Armstrong and Buzz Aldrin on the moon in 1969 could not, in conscience, feel good about its technical genius while coming up short on its social obligations. Looking the other way while 12 percent of our population was being punished because their skin was black instead of white simply became unacceptable. Justice, though a little late, was arriving.

Similarly, it had become time to point out the societal limits imposed on women. It wasn't fair that half of the population was being held back because of the arrangement of their chromosomes from jobs they wanted, from political office, from educational preferences, and from stopping off at a bar for a drink, unescorted, if the mood hit them.

The Civil Rights struggle was gifted with articulate leaders. Speeches by Martin Luther King Jr., Jesse Jackson, Julian Bond, and others could rouse followers to action. The injustice of race discrimination was portrayed with emotion, clarity, and intensity, all accompanied by an impassioned plea to take up the cause.

Though women did not have a roster of communicators who could inspire crowds to action in the same dramatic way, we had leaders nonetheless.

Betty Friedan recruited feminists with her 1963 book *The Feminine Mystique,* which became a controversial bestseller just when controversy was needed. She wrote of subtle forms of discrimination, pointing out that women were the victims of a system of delusions and false values compelling them to find fulfillment through unrestricted devotion to husband and children.

She didn't wait long to make her point. In chapter one, she said, "Over and over women heard in voices of tradition and Freudian sophistication that they could desire no greater destiny than to glory in their own femininity and to pity the neurotic, unfeminine, unhappy women who wanted to be poets or physicians or presidents."

In 1971 Germaine Greer would stir some consciousness with *The Female Eunuch*. Kate Millett in 1969 would make the case for shared parenting by saying "The care of children . . . is infinitely better left to the best-trained practitioners of both sexes . . . rather than to harried and all too frequently unhappy persons with little time or taste for the work of educating minds however young or beloved." That was from her book *Sexual Politics*, which pulled no punches in examining the inherited family roles of society.

Gloria Steinem, a woman I know and admire, may have come the closest to having a voice people paid attention to, no matter how blunt she might be in a given situation. Asked in an interview for *Writer's Digest* to define "women's work," Gloria responded with seven memorable words—"The definition of women's work is shitwork."

There were others who wrote with passion about the need for women to stand up and say, "Enough!" And singer Helen Reddy delivered a song called "I Am Woman" with lyrics that urged women to replace their wishbone with a backbone.

I remember my college graduation day. I was a nervous wreck, not because of the ceremony but because my father was the commencement speaker. I felt the familiar mixture of pride and terror at what he might say. My pride was justified, my fear unfounded. His talk was wonderful and so was the college experience. My new freedom, many friendships, and countless adventures provided a huge building block for the future.

I couldn't help feeling that as soon as I moved to New York City I would find a job that would put an exclamation point on the freedom I had felt during that year in France. Maybe then I could become involved in what appeared to be an emerging awareness among some—not all—women about the importance of opportunities and choice in women's lives.

I had a good education and high hopes for a rewarding job in New York. I was about to find out what the real world was like for women at that time.

CHAPTER 5

Are "Conforming" and "Confining" the Same Word in a Woman's Dictionary?

No one forgets his or her first job. The first kiss may evaporate in your memory, but not the first time someone actually chose you over other applicants, trusted you with an assignment, promised you a paycheck for what you did. When my time came to enter the world of paid employment, what I wasn't prepared for was that men would be making all the decisions.

When I was in Spain during the summer following my junior year abroad in college, I went to Pamplona for the running of the bulls. The planned stampede takes place annually at the Festival of San Fermin, where the bulls are turned loose in the street and people run with them, doing their best to avoid being trampled by thundering hooves or gored by sharp horns.

It's a little like a 50 percent off sale at a department store the day after Thanksgiving.

The people who jump into the midst of this Pamplona mayhem are mostly young, often influenced by wine, and certifiably examples that at times in our lives the porch light in on, but there's no one home.

You have to be a daredevil to do this, or you have to be a visiting college girl eager to sample what the world far away from Virginia had to offer.

I survived the silliness undamaged and reminded myself that there are some things in life you don't need to do twice. In fact, I celebrated my twenty-first birthday during those crazy days, and figured I was now truly an adult.

In retrospect, running with the bulls in Pamplona was exhilarating. Job-hunting in New York was something else.

The first sharp turn in my learning curve of life was just ahead.

I already had a place to live. I would be moving in with three other young women on New York's upper West side, between Central Park West and Amsterdam Avenue. Two of my apartment mates had something in common. They both had jobs. And the third roommate, my longtime friend Emily Squires, found one quickly. I didn't, but I was sure that employers in the big city would be impressed with my academic credentials and ready to hire me.

Some were. But not for the kind of work I was seeking. I had no intention of becoming a secretary. It was a fine profession and many secretaries who stayed with a firm for a long time had a certain kind of power around their office, mostly derived from their own longevity and their supervisor's position on the organizational chart.

I was vaguely interested in public relations or advertising, or both, although I looked at other possibilities. I could write a coherent sentence. I told myself I had a decent flair for creativity. Certainly I was in the right town. New York City was home base for many of the nation's advertising and public relations giants.

Rejection became routine. Each day I'd return to the apartment still unemployed. The "can-you-type" offers were plentiful, but I was holding out for something where I felt I had a fair chance at developing a career doing what I thought I would enjoy at a level where I felt I could influence outcomes.

I began to fear that no one was taking me seriously. I heard all the standard lines:

"We're looking for someone with a little more experience."
"We'll keep your resume on file and if anything opens up, we'll call you."
"Have you considered the typing pool as a way of getting started?"

My carefully constructed visions of life after college were disintegrating. I had prepared myself for an atmosphere that included a good job with a prominent company; the independent lifestyle of a young woman enjoying the pace of the world's greatest city; the triumph of demonstrating to my parents that I could take care of myself.

That's when I learned my first lesson about the real world—no one was as eager to hire an early-twenties person with a good academic background as I thought they would be. Particularly if that person was a woman.

My roommates were concerned about me. I was concerned about me. My father, getting ever more prominent in Congress, was concerned. That's when I learned lesson number two.

It was my introduction to the actual application of "it's not *what* you know, but *who* you know."

Today it has a more sophisticated label. It's called "networking." In a climate that is drowning in job placement firms and human resources organizations, still the most effective hiring happens when people in high places pick up the phone and dial 1-800-UOME, as in "you owe me."

My father made that call to a gentleman named Don Thompson at N. W. Ayer and Son, Inc., an outstanding advertising and public relations enterprise (think Mad Men!).

I had mixed emotions about his intervention. One part of me resented it, because I was determined to get a job on my own. The other part of me welcomed his influence because I was tired and humiliated by being turned down.

I'm glad the "other part" won.

I had my first job. It came with the title "account assistant" and paid $80 a week. The door had been opened for me. I now had a chance to prove what I could do, to make myself valuable.

To this day, that is still what women in the workplace need most—opportunity and appreciation of their qualifications, which may be nontraditional, so they can compete fairly. That's what this elusive thing called "equality" really is—that's why it's called "equal opportunity."

Four message-carrying memories have endured from that first working experience in New York. Each helped shape how I would approach the rest of my life and the things I wanted to change.

My first discovery was that most of the people who made it possible for me to move ahead were men. They were in charge. They had power. Still, they didn't have to go to bat for me.

I was assigned to assist four men who handled four very different accounts. I was ambitious, willing to work hard on the little things in order to earn the right to be a part of larger projects. Each of them taught me important skills—how to write a press release, how to handle clients—and gave me opportunities beyond my job description.

Before long, I was promoted and my bosses asked me to stage events and trusted me to take on more responsibility with major accounts like the 1964 New York World's Fair and the visit of the Hope Diamond to the United States. I liked working with men.

The message: Hard work pays off and leadership respect is gender-neutral.

The second discovery was that New York City is a long way from Lynchburg, Virginia.

No one around the office looked like me. I was the only female White Anglo-Saxon Protestant in my department. In my prior life, including college, people like me were the norm. At N. W. Ayer I was surrounded by the genuine realization of a word that social scientists had not yet adopted—diversity.

There were men and women of all backgrounds, races, and religions. This was the America I knew existed but had not yet met. I developed many new friendships and the surroundings at N. W. Ayer provided a stimulating cross-section of people I was overdue to meet. I had not realized the extent of my insularity—except for my brief escape to Europe—until then.

The message: If we want to experience fully the richness of life and of our nation, we have to be willing to move beyond our familiar surroundings.

My third New York discovery was how thrilled I was with my first paycheck. I went immediately to a store and bought a dress (it was green). Though it was hardly expensive, it was the first time I had ever purchased anything with my own earned income.

That moment was symbolic. It was a baby step toward following the advice of my father's frequent lectures to me about being financially independent. "Have a bank account of your own," he would say. With what was left over after buying my dress, I opened one. And this time I knew the monthly statements would come to me.

The message: Married or single, women need a checkbook of their own.

My fourth discovery was that I could not tolerate discrimination. I can live with unhappiness, but not with injustice.

I think I have always felt this way. Discrimination in matters of race, religion, gender, class, sexual orientation—all of the denigrating labels people assign to those who are not "just like them"—I find abhorrent.

Why do people need to put others down to lift themselves up? What is it that prevents people from measuring others by the same standards they gauge themselves?

A particularly unpleasant memory from my early New York years still troubles me.

When I was at N. W. Ayer, one of the people I got to know was a young man from Baltimore who worked in the mailroom named Jack. He was

African American. We became good friends, and when I was preparing to get married in early 1965, I invited him to my wedding.

Then I learned that the church in Alexandria, Virginia, where the wedding was to take place, did not allow black people to attend. I was shocked. I was also twenty-three. The more mature me would have raised hell about this, moved the wedding to another site, or called the whole thing off.

I had to tell Jack that he couldn't come. I was horrified. But what was even worse was that he was not surprised. He graciously told me he couldn't come anyway.

The message: To maintain your self-respect it is better to upset people by doing what you know is right. In the years since this incident, I have always tried to do that.

My two years in New York were a proving ground to show that I could compete professionally. It was a challenging place and time which rewarded success and was unforgiving with failure.

Just as with the bulls in Pamplona, if you didn't know how to deal with New York, you ran the risk of getting run over. I learned to face the reality of the workplace, to understand hierarchy, to deliver what was expected, and as women must, to do a little more.

New York was no longer new to me, but marriage was. It was time to explore what Amelia Earhart called "that attractive cage."

CHAPTER 6

How Can We Redefine Power?

"Speak softly and carry a big stick" is a might-makes-right approach to power. I think women look at power differently. Having often been on the receiving end of its abuse, women have pretty much arrived at a quiet consensus that power is best used to bring about change—positive change, peacefully achieved. That's what eventual equality will produce—a softer use of power. Macho will be balanced out with mellow.

Power and illusion are awkward companions.

For centuries women had only the power that was rationed out reluctantly by men. In place of power, women substituted illusion, existing on a blend of fantasy to supplement the small scraps of decision-making that they were allotted.

It was easy to confuse responsibility with power. They are not the same. Responsibility for homemaking and child rearing is front-loaded with obligation, but shallow on opportunity.

Marriage is a high-visibility example of power acquisition and distribution. People fall in love, get married, and then frequently find they've traded independence for limited choices.

Amelia Earhart is remembered as America's most famous female aviator. Stirred by the belief that "women can conquer flight just as well as men," she pioneered world records over both the Atlantic and Pacific oceans. Until her disappearance on an around-the-world flight in 1937, her feats of daring were anticipated with high expectations.

Her leadership was not confined to the cockpit. She was decades ahead in creating a version of a premarital contract, making it clear to her husband, George Palmer Putnam, that their marriage would be a fifty-fifty arrangement.

On her wedding day, February 7, 1931, at the age of thirty-three, Amelia Earhart handed her groom-to-be a letter that included the following stipulations:

> *You must know again my reluctance to marry, my feeling that I shatter thereby chances in work which mean so much to me . . .*
>
> *Please let us not interfere with each other's work or play, nor let the world see private joys or disagreements. In this connection I may have to keep some place where I can go to be myself now and then, for I cannot guarantee to endure at all times the confinements of even an attractive cage.*
>
> *I must exact a cruel promise, and this is that you will let me go in a year if we find no happiness together. I will try to do my best in every way.*

In later years her husband paid tribute to the Earhart letter by terming it "brutal in its frankness, but beautiful in its honesty."

What she seemed to be communicating in words that left little doubt as to her intent was that two conditions were important to her and she was not going to permit the marriage ceremony to diminish either one.

One condition was the continuation of her career. She liked aviation. She was very good at it. She saw no reason to put either her skill or her passion on the shelf.

Her second condition was to make no compromise with honesty. The letter itself echoes with the message of how greatly she valued integrity.

Critics have said her tone was selfish, that she failed in not conceding that marriage requires a woman to give up some of her goals, to sacrifice some of her ambition. Amelia Earhart's letter clearly asks, "Why?"

Although the idea may be counter to the traditional emotions of the wedding ritual, there are volumes to be said for having an understanding of "shared power" before you call the caterer.

If you're going to have a partner, that partner ought to respect your freedom, your wish to express yourself outside the home. In my own marriage, it has always been understood that Paul and I are true partners who share responsibilities. When our children were born, he was in the delivery room—which was highly unusual at that time—and we have shared parenting roles comfortably. Throughout our marriage, I have continued to make my own decisions about my life, and I have maintained my financial independence so I would never be trapped as so many married women have been.

I have noticed that couples who marry for the second or third time tend to make a deal—to agree from the start that the other party has certain rights and should have the freedom to exercise them. The "deal" between Paul and me occurred naturally and has always been implicit.

Coming out of college in the '60s I didn't think a lot about power, except to observe that men had most of it. In my family, my mother had influence, but my father had power. I went to an all-women's college, but the president of the college was a man.

When it came time to look for a job, I just naturally figured that my interviews would be with men. They were.

Power should be gender-neutral. It should be earned. It should be exercised with care. If not inhaled in small quantities it can go to one's head.

I've been in positions of leadership for over thirty years, but I had never thought of myself as being powerful, mostly because the causes I was championing were always more powerful than I was.

The question came up after my U.S. Senate campaign as I was speaking about that experience to a women's group in Philadelphia. I was asked, "Did you feel powerful?" I answered, "*Sometimes.*" Later, I thought a lot about that question.

The influence that I had as a potential member of the nation's highest legislative body meant that people listened to what I had to say; they cared about my views and values on a wide range of topics.

That was what I came to think of as "the power of possibility" or "the possibility of power." If people agreed with my positions on an issue, they could expect to have me as an advocate to make it happen. And while some politicians have changed the positions they took as candidates after they were elected, I believe many thought I could be trusted to remain consistent.

I was unwilling to say something I did not believe. A case in point was an early phone conversation I had with well-known Democratic political consultant, James Carville, who asked me about my position on the death penalty.

At that time, 1992, in Pennsylvania, polls showed that the majority of voters favored capital punishment. But I definitely did not and that's what I told Carville. He asked, "Have you ever said that in public?" and when I said no, he replied, "Then I advise you to pray about it."

I would not change my views to accommodate the polls, and I'm sure some votes were lost.

But back to the power question, running for public office, assuming you are a legitimate candidate, provides an excellent platform for educating the public on issues you care about. My advocacy for women, and firsthand knowledge of so many challenges women face, from my Women's Way days, gave me a powerful voice in that high-profile campaign.

I used to have a sign in my office that read, "Everyone has a right to my opinion." Before I ran for office, few people cared what I thought, but in 1992 my opinion was of interest to millions of Pennsylvania voters. I think that's power.

One of the observations I made early in life while watching people in power was that most of them had arrived where they were because of a special talent or a willingness to take a risk at the right time. Most leaders, men and women, also simply work hard.

Power can either intimidate you or invite you.

One of the stories from history that I like to share, particularly with young girls, is about a teenager who lived nearly two hundred years ago in England.

This nineteen-year-old girl named Mary had shown some modest writing ability and was asked to enter a contest involving the composition of a ghost story. She checked out the other people in the competition, some of them already established writers, and immediately concluded she was over her head.

Before she officially declined, she sought the advice of some adults in her life, and they suggested she had nothing to lose by trying (a parallel to my father's frequent recitation of "somebody said it couldn't be done . . . but she would be one who wouldn't say so 'til she tried.").

So Mary made the decision to go ahead. The night of her decision, she had a nightmare and woke up terrified. Having no other idea for a ghost story, she simply wrote about her nightmare. As it turned out, she was the only competitor to submit her story on time.

Mary Shelley gave it the one-word title *Frankenstein*.

Women, who have rarely enjoyed the attainment of power in American history, now have the opportunity to avoid the problems that accompany its acquisition. As we study the characteristics of leaders, more and more of whom are female in the twenty-first century, we can treat the exercise like a buffet table, choosing only those traits that will utilize power in its most positive fashion.

In my campaign, I remember so well the words of an unemployed laborer in Blair County, Pennsylvania. He gave me as sound a slice of advice about politicians as anyone could, summing it up in five words, "Don't become one of them!"

That's the opportunity. Women have a chance to avoid the arrogance that getting to the top—or even part way there—can bring on.

The principal symptom of that loss of humility is separation from the very issues you had to overcome to get yourself into a position of leadership—separation from your identity as an agent of change and separation from unity with other women who share similar dreams of fulfilling their potential.

It's the opposite of Lily Tomlin's comment when she said, "We're all in this alone." When it comes to justice and social reform, women can do more as a team than we can ever hope to accomplish as individuals. We create our own cocoons when we isolate ourselves and almost certainly resign ourselves to a lifestyle dictated by others.

I didn't consider all this about the value of unity among women when I was a newlywed.

Those ideas were not formed yet for me in the midsixties, but I left New York with one thing certain—my confidence in my own ability. Paul and I were heading south. Surely, I would have my choice of good jobs in Philadelphia.

I couldn't wait.

Hello, Philadelphia!

CHAPTER 7

Whose Expectations Are They Anyway?

If you look in the mirror every morning and ask yourself, "Is everything in my world the way it ought to be?" and the answer is "no," I believe what you are looking at is opportunity. Traditional expectations for women, relayed for centuries from one generation to the next, had constricted women's choices and deprived the nation of their contributions. I was impatient with the pace of change.

Leaving Virginia for New York City had been a dramatic change in surroundings for me. Moving from New York after my marriage was almost as dramatic in its cultural impact. My first night in our suburban Philadelphia apartment was a sleepless one because it was so quiet outside. The crickets actually kept me awake.

I knew Philadelphia only slightly, having visited some of Paul's college friends who'd settled there. Most of my knowledge of the city itself was selectively stored in my memory from history class, where it had been drilled into my mind that this is where America got its start in 1776.

I had heard jokes about Philadelphia being a rest stop between bustling New York and powerful Washington, two cities I had already experienced.

Philadelphia, I was told, was a place heavily flavored with yesteryear—the Liberty Bell, Independence Hall, Valley Forge. It was a city proud of its past and quite reluctant to leave it behind.

One of the people I met early on, during my job search there, was Thacher Longstreth, then president of the Chamber of Commerce, who held almost legend status as a Philadelphian. With great affection, he loved to refer to the "city of brotherly love, and sisterly restraint."

Given this introduction, I would not have predicted that I would come to love Philadelphia or that it would become, in the forty years ahead, such a key battleground in a new revolution, the somewhat-spontaneous, somewhat-synchronized surge to overthrow habits and laws that had for so long controlled the lives of women.

After two years of apartment living, Paul and I settled in Rosemont, a suburb in the midst of what is called Philadelphia's "Main Line," a stretch of communities west of the city along the railroad line. It's a place where old money intersects with the new, where it was popular to joke about the Main Line Unemployment Office having valet parking.

It was there that I would discover the elusive definition of "home." Not so much discover it, but create it.

To me, "home" is where you can return no matter where life's pushing and pulling have taken you. It's where you can find comfort away from the frantic pace of the rest of your life, even when that turbulent pace is something you helped create.

"Home" is not so much a building, though I grew to love every room, every nuance, and every blemish in our house. Instead, "home" is a place to rally your family, reclaim your energy, and pack your emotional luggage for the next challenge. It's a place to claim your personal space, like Virginia Wolff's "A Room of Her Own."

After experiencing Virginia, New York and countries overseas, it was Rosemont that deserved my label of "home." No matter what would happen in the next forty years—no matter how intense my public combat with established forces became; no matter how turbulent the political phase of my life turned out to be; no matter how much controversy was stirred as I called attention to the injustice of systems restricting women's rights and opportunities—I always knew that my home would provide peace and promise I would find nowhere else.

"Home" meant proximity to the arts and culture of Philadelphia, although I found myself attending too many events out of a sense of obligation, and I paid for this miscalculation in terms of wasted time and social malaise.

"Home" meant the intimacy of small shops in neighboring towns where people knew each others' names and the service and quality were always high.

"Home" meant physical security, a sort of mythically safe distance from big city crime, despite the fact that our home was burglarized four times and I took each incident as a severe violation of my personal space and property. The police kept advising us to get a dog, and finally we did.

The geography we had chosen contributed other substantial gifts to my concept of "home."

After trying out several area congregations—I had grown up a Methodist and attended an Episcopal school for twelve years—I found a church which, beyond being a place of inspiration and tranquility, had a large congregation whose members were leaders of the region and whose mission was focused on the community at large. Unwilling to isolate the agenda to its suburban congregation, Bryn Mawr Presbyterian Church also reached out with an arm that extended to the needy in the big city and around the world.

Also prominent in my definition of Rosemont as "home" was a public school system ideally suited to educating our two children, Courtney and Paul. The public school district was well-funded, had first-class facilities, and was staffed by professionals who were eager to teach there and competed for the privilege of working in its positive learning atmosphere.

My thrill at finding a great school for my kids was tempered by a question that wouldn't go away: why can't all schools be as good as this one? A few miles from where we lived, in overcrowded, understaffed classrooms, thousands of Philadelphia girls and boys faced much greater odds against getting an education that would lead to solid careers, fulfilled lives and a better chance to succeed than their parents had.

When I was growing up, I was expected to get a good education, including a college degree, and to become a wife. That was an implicit, and sometimes explicit, goal. Develop your mind, but also your social skills and in the event you fail on the husband front, have some basic secretarial skills so you can get a job.

Those were the expectations that made women finally begin to ask, "Is that all there is?"

I don't enjoy cooking. I don't pretend to, and I'm lucky that my husband is a better cook than I am. I applaud those who find satisfaction in homemaking, but it's not for me. At a very early age I wanted to accomplish something significant outside the home, and I did not want to apologize for whatever was the achievement.

There was never any question in my mind that women could do the same work as men did. I had read about what happened during World War II. "Men only" factory jobs were quickly turned over to women when men marched off to war. Farms, businesses, schools—all of the previously male-dominated pursuits—were to some degree guided by women.

A spark happened there. Women, many of them for the first time, picked up a paycheck of their own. It was a new experience. They were no longer on an allowance. They had control of the family money and had to make decisions on how it was spent.

When the war ended, the men came back to reclaim the jobs, and the women retreated to home duties they had never really left, because during the war they had learned how to manage a job outside the home while still keeping the household, raising the children.

A core of women remembered the responsible jobs they had and those paychecks with their names on them. This helped keep a faint flame of independence flickering for women during the '50s. They had been tested, and they had proven themselves.

In the fall of 1965, I entered the Philadelphia job market and found much the same problem I had faced in New York in landing a professional job. This was especially disappointing because my former employer made introductions for me and wrote glowing letters of recommendation. The fact that I was now a married woman made some employers more timid, fearing an oncoming pregnancy.

I recall being turned down by one potential employer who said, "We're not ready for a woman at this level." When I met him by chance years later, I actually thanked him for setting me on my career path. The hurt and anger I had felt upon that rejection led me in the direction of fighting sex discrimination.

I did eventually get a good job in the Public Affairs department at Smith Kline & French Laboratories, a large pharmaceutical firm, where I soon earned a promotion and was making more money than Paul and most of the other men we knew. But I had to leave that job in 1967 because company policy required that women resign when they reached six months of pregnancy. Family and Medical Leave legislation was years away and everyone assumed—including me—that I would stay home and raise my children.

Courtney Lynn Yeakel was born in September 1967 and Paul Mann Yeakel Jr. arrived in March 1969. They were both beautiful, wonderful children, and my center shifted, as I think every mother's does, when they entered my life. I had my hands full with two babies less than eighteen months apart, and Paul was busy building his investment business.

When children are born, parents envision them growing up to live happy and fulfilling personal and professional lives. There is a generational incentive that spurs you to try to parent better than those who tended the family tree before you.

That challenge entitles you to learn all you can, to make your own mistakes, and to glory in how precious the memories become. Courtney and Paul Jr. would go on to achieve lives that have made us proud and to produce children who, in their time, will add branches to the tree, continuing what I call "the obligation of example."

It was difficult for a woman to make long-range career plans when at almost every turn her vision was narrowed by reminders of her biological reality and her limited choices outside the home. Meanwhile, men were—as they are now—encouraged to expand their ambitions.

Real confidence comes from knowing your strengths and believing you will have a fair chance to use and develop them. I think I like baseball. I don't know much about the game, but what I do know—that it has rules, the bases are the same distance apart for everyone, everybody gets three strikes—sounds fair to me. Baseball was seldom taught to girls.

Every woman I knew in the early 1970s had more to contribute than her domestic skills, and many wanted a larger sphere of influence. Finding out what that influence could be was as exciting as it was evolutionary.

CHAPTER 8

How Is Profit Defined in a Nonprofit World?

There exists a popular myth that when you aren't qualified for a "real" job, you turn to nonprofit work. Anyone who thinks that way has never worked through the night on a sink-or-swim funding proposal, or experienced the agility required to manage an operation on a shoestring, or run to the mailbox to see if the check really is in the mail. Worse yet, they haven't distinguished between "something to do" and something that needs doing.

I had never considered joining the Junior League, much less becoming its president. I regarded the organization as primarily social and a place for privileged women who had time on their hands.

I was wrong, at least as far as the Junior League of Philadelphia was concerned.

The invitation to join the Junior League came at just the right moment for me. I needed something beyond my parenting and household management responsibilities and I missed the office environment. I was impatient at gatherings of couples where men clustered in one corner, women in another.

I often talked to the men because they were discussing topics I was interested in—politics, business, and world affairs. For the most part, the women exchanged information about daily challenges, including children's issues. It wasn't that I didn't care about those things. I was just hungry for more stimulating conversation.

I did not go quietly through my Junior League years. I signed up for every available training course. I accepted opportunities to assume leadership roles, chairing the Goodwill Thrift Shop and Education Committees, starting a Wanted Child Committee to focus on reproductive rights, taking on three vice presidential appointments, and attending a handful of out-of-town conferences.

One of those events, in the late 1970s, was in Kansas City where the Association of Junior Leagues of America debated whether to take a position on the ratification of the Equal Rights Amendment, an attempt to ensure and protect women's rights under the U.S. Constitution.

History will show that the amendment came up two states short and therefore technically failed. I have never accepted that result as a loss because the value of the attention the ERA campaign generated in the press and among the public served to put the inequities and injustices toward women in a spotlight bright enough to give gender equality a foothold on the American conscience.

Opponents railed that ERA supporters were radicals, bra burners, man haters, and even advocates of unisex toilets. We saw it differently. We were merely seeking to have women covered by the same umbrella of freedom that the Constitution had provided for men. Although time ran out in the ratification process before victory could be achieved, the entire ERA initiative proved to be a wake-up call for women—and a number of supportive men—all across the nation.

Among my earlier experiences that had opened the door for my passion about this cause was the unforgettable two years I had spent as a volunteer counseling women with unplanned pregnancies. I had gotten involved through a church in my neighborhood. I became a volunteer options counselor with CHOICE, a program to help pregnant girls and women get the services they needed. It took me to a part of life I had barely glimpsed before.

CHOICE was an acronym for Concern for Health Options: Information, Care, and Education. It grew out of the statewide Clergy Consultation Service in the early 1970s before the *Roe v. Wade* Supreme Court decision legalizing abortion.

Every Monday afternoon I showed up at the Booth Maternity Center, a Salvation Army hospital with a pregnancy-testing clinic. When the women and girls who came for testing learned they were pregnant and thus found themselves in difficult or desperate situations, they could meet with a CHOICE counselor.

I saw girls as young as twelve—some with their horrified mothers—and women as old as forty-five, single, married, and divorced. They came from many different races, from different social and economic levels. They all shared two conditions—they were pregnant, and they needed help.

It was my responsibility to provide information to these women about their options in order to help them make their decisions. Once they decided on their course of action, I was there to support them.

I often became an intermediary, pleading with a physician or a hospital to see a client who had no money. Sometimes I would work with a woman to raise the money to go to a New York City clinic where early outpatient abortions were performed safely and legally under that state's laws.

At other times I assisted those who decided to continue the pregnancy and needed advice on adoption services or housing. Some of the most emotional parts of counseling were the interventions with parents, spouses or boyfriends, particularly in cases where teenagers had been thrown out of their homes in disgrace.

I remembered a friend in high school who had confided in me that she had undergone an abortion at fifteen, but did so in a New York hospital while supported by her family, who were able to pay $2,000 for the procedure. I contrasted that to another memory of a twenty-six-year-old friend, with limited resources, who had an unsafe and illegal procedure and became sterile as a result of the infection she developed.

Witnessing the indignities faced by women with unintended pregnancies and economic inequities reinforced my belief that women must have the fundamental right to make personal, private decisions about their own lives and reproductive health. Women must be free to decide when and whether to have children.

The issue was controversial in the 1970s and it still is. Emotions run high. Religion is a factor. I respect other people's rights to their own opinions and personal choices, and I ask that others respect those differences and do not attempt to impose their views on the rest of us.

When a young attorney from Texas, Sarah Weddington, successfully argued *Roe v. Wade* before the U.S. Supreme Court in 1972, the court's decision acknowledged the right of a woman to choose abortion, and to do so legally.

My prochoice position would follow me through some of the toughest battles still to be waged in speaking for women, including my public attempts to raise funds for women's organizations, and my campaign for the U.S. Senate.

The decade I spent as an active member of the Junior League of Philadelphia confirmed my commitment to service and advocacy, and it convinced me that I could not sit on the sidelines in the struggle for women's rights. My experience there also clarified and strengthened my leadership capabilities.

Whatever I was in, I wanted to lead it, and I almost always was asked to do that.

After holding a number of high profile positions in the organization, I was selected by the nominating committee for the first vice president position, which meant automatic succession to the presidency.

I accepted and soon learned that a petition candidate was going to challenge me. She represented a more conservative part of the membership and the choice between us was fairly clear. I felt boosted by my win, which came on a platform of action, urging the membership to concentrate its energy on external community activities.

That's why most nonprofit organizations exist, to improve the communities around them. Sometimes that's done by helping individuals who are underserved. Sometimes it's done by widening the cultural opportunities.

Running a nonprofit is not a job for sissies. I've never regarded any segment of that service world as a rest home for the underachiever. To me, it is a valuable professional lifestyle for people who understand the challenge the late Senator Robert Kennedy issued so often, to "not just see things as they are and ask: 'why' . . . but to dream things that never were and ask: 'why not'?"

Many of the skills that are required to be chief executive of a large company or the head of a governmental department are the same skills needed to develop a nonprofit's strategic plan and to deliver successful outcomes. When the CEO of a business fails, she or he is either replaced or the business goes under. It's no different in the nonprofit world. Boards of directors require similar accountability.

I've never had to look far to find nonprofit executives with the kind of talent that inspires.

For years I admired the leadership of the late Anne d'Harnoncourt, who took a struggling Philadelphia Museum of Art, rallied enormous financial support, attracted an amazing string of art exhibits from around the world, and made the museum a renowned center of culture and pride. Her no-nonsense business style, combined with her personal grace and superb understanding of her field, demonstrated qualifications that could have seated her comfortably at the head of the table of business board rooms all over America.

And I didn't have to look far to see the managerial genius of Sister Mary Scullion, a woman of extraordinary purpose and professionalism, who was named by *Time* magazine in 2009 as one of the most influential women in the United States. Sister Mary's guidance of Project HOME is devoted to the people who were left behind in the rollercoaster of urban life. She houses the homeless, provides jobs, training opportunities and other programs to help women, men and young people who are trying to turn their lives around. Whether it's five-year plans, cash flow, or a return-on-investment that can be measured in human dividends, she is an executive of spectacular credentials.

Anne and Mary are only two among thousands that I could list. When someone asks "Where's the profit in nonprofit organizations?" I invite them to imagine a community without them. If all of America's nonprofit and volunteer initiatives disappeared, the gaps in a community's life would be wide and the impact incalculable.

I was ready for leadership responsibility and the cause I believed in had become apparent—doing what I could do to help women gain access to the power we had been denied for so long. That cause was worth whatever I could bring to it.

The biggest challenge for all nonprofits is raising money and for women's organizations that has been especially true.

Generosity is an American trait. Americans did not invent the art of giving, but we took it to a level of value and sophistication that the world had never seen. However, men have historically made most of the money and most of the giving decisions.

Fundraising became very sophisticated in the second half of the twentieth century. The population grew and with it the needs of a community. In the 1970s in Philadelphia the special problems faced by women—domestic violence and sexual assault, employment discrimination, economic, health, and legal inequities—prompted the emergence of an increasing number of support organizations.

Their financial needs were substantial. A collision course was inevitable between those who had the money and those who needed it. What happened rallied women as never before.

CHAPTER 9

If We Can See the Power of One, Can We Imagine the Power of Many?

> No matter who you aspire to be, or what you choose to do, the option is there for you to feel good about your decision. What enhances that feeling is when you find others who feel the same way you do.

I've always liked the idea of coalitions.

It seems obvious to me that if one person with a purpose can make progress toward a goal, more people working toward the same end can get there faster. The unity of many voices makes the message louder—and the louder the message the more likely it is to improve the hearing of those you're trying to reach.

A coalition at its best takes on difficult problems and solves them. It advocates for its members and demonstrates the strength of numbers. The whole adventure of civilization assumes our willingness to work together. When we do, we all prosper.

The AARP is an excellent example of the potential impact of a coalition. A few people who understood that extended life expectancy presented challenges and opportunities eventually became the American Association of Retired Persons and snowballed into a national phenomenon.

What may have started out as an effort to get senior citizen discounts on bus fares and movie tickets has grown into the most powerful lobby knocking on Washington's Congressional doors and making itself heard as a bloc of voters at election time.

In the area of fundraising for social service agencies, the idea of the United Way was always a good one. It provided a vehicle for individuals and companies to contribute to worthwhile nonprofit groups.

Instead of multiple health and human service organizations pursuing the same donors, why not permit people to contribute to a single entity that would distribute those funds to the separate nonprofits?

In the 1970s in Philadelphia, the United Way had a strong corporate base. The payroll deduction system, introduced by the Internal Revenue Service during World War II, had been adopted to make employee giving relatively painless. Research showed that contributors would triple their charitable gifts this way.

Millions of dollars poured into the United Way. The annual pledge drive, heavily fueled by publicity, produced suspense each year as a publicized thermometer informed the public of how close the campaign was to its goal. Historically, a surge of pledges in the final days of the drive put it over the top. The bands played. The balloons soared. The city felt good for another year.

But something else was happening in Philadelphia during this time.

With a growing public awareness of crises in the lives of women, new organizations were forming to confront each of the problems and address unmet needs.

To function, they needed money. When they asked donors, they frequently heard "I gave at the office," and they were advised to see the United Way. They did, and were told that they were too small or too controversial to be United Way members.

The creation of Women's Way was revolutionary on several levels. Initially incorporated as the Philadelphia Women's Coalition in 1976 and funded with a start-up grant from the visionary William Penn Foundation, Womens Way (a marketing brand with apostrophe intentionally left out) was formed by seven organizations providing services to women in the Philadelphia region. They joined forces to raise money for all their programs.

One unique aspect of the coalition was that these groups had been competing for scarce funds in a climate where "women's issues" were marginalized by traditional funders, including the United Way. The seven nonprofits, which addressed women's legal problems, employment barriers, health concerns, rape crisis treatment, economic, and other inequities turned over precious, carefully cultivated donor lists, signed a contract to define their mutual commitment, put their leaders on a common board of directors, and developed an innovative objective formula for allocating funds raised.

I was involved at the outset as chair of the CHOICE Board when the first meeting was convened. It was an extraordinary and inspiring idea from the beginning.

There were two aspects to the Women's Way mission. One was meeting the survival needs of the member organizations that formed the coalition. The other was responding to the desire of donors, especially women, to support causes they cared about. The second emphasis was the concept of a Women's Way founder, Louise Lewis Page, to create a vehicle for charitable giving to organizations addressing the special needs of women. Louise helped persuade her friend Allen Bacon at the William Penn Foundation to support this new venture, and she recruited his wife, Margaret Bacon, whose biography of Lucretia Mott (*Valiant Friend*) was soon to be published, to join the Women's Way Board.

We launched Women's Way's first fundraising campaign in the spring of 1977. I was the volunteer campaign chair and made that initial presentation with a modest slide show we had created. It was clear right away that women would respond to the compelling needs of other women and to our coalition approach.

One year later we held our first major fundraising event, presenting the newly established Lucretia Mott Award to Coretta Scott King. Over four hundred people attended the dinner, which in just a decade would become the largest event of its kind in the region.

To show we were serious about getting the money we raised "on the street" where it was needed right away, we began the allocation process immediately, distributing $25,000 to the members in June 1977, just three months after the fundraising campaign began. We continued that pattern annually, giving essentially all the money we raised each year to the agencies. This was a high-risk decision but paid off in many ways.

I became the second chair of the Women's Way Board, following the legendary Ernesta Drinker Ballard, who opened numerous doors to the fledgling coalition through her multiple contacts. We all worked extremely hard to create a new model of collaboration that was innovative and inclusive.

We created a Discretionary Fund, to make small grants to nonmember agencies serving women, and we began admitting new members in the early eighties. Each new organization was required to have a demonstrated base of community support, an advocacy component, and a willingness to give up most of its fundraising activity and work with the coordinated campaign.

We never imagined anything but success. We saw ourselves as a permanent organization representing a largely neglected 52 percent of the population. Women's Way (which recently put the apostrophe back) will celebrate its thirty-fifth anniversary in 2012.

To succeed, a coalition requires four cornerstones:

- An uncluttered purpose—goals that are understandable and attainable;
- An uncommon strategy—a decisive set of plans and deadlines with enough flexibility to adapt to unanticipated change;
- An unselfish team—people who trust their leaders and each other and are willing to put cooperation ahead of personal gain;
- An unwavering belief—the conviction that the value of the mission is worth the commitment each member must make to achieve it.

When I became executive director (later called president and CEO) of Women's Way in 1980, I had no illusion that this would be easy. The United Way was the ten-ton elephant in the room and we were the ant. As one of my friends said, "Women's Way bites you on the ankle." The confrontation and controversy had already begun when I took over the leadership.

We had a couple of things going for us. One was unity, and when women are unified in their purpose, change will not be far behind. The other was a growing community awareness that many important agencies, including those in the Women's Way coalition, were not included in the United Way "family."

CHAPTER 10

Why Is the Door to Opportunity for Women Often Marked "Push?"

The bumblebee analogy should be required reading for women leaders. Engineering calculations conclude that the bumblebee cannot possibly fly. It's designed all wrong aerodynamically. The body is too large. The wings are too small. Every time it takes off, it should plunge back to earth. Fortunately, the bumblebee does not understand its technical limitations, and it's a good thing it doesn't or we'd be living in a world of plastic flowers. Believing you can accomplish what others say you can't—that's part of being a woman, and most of being a fundraiser.

Women's capacity for achievement has seldom been accurately estimated. Most women I've met have no idea what they are capable of accomplishing.

That condition has led me to the conclusion that a woman's contribution to society is directly proportional to the amount of encouragement she receives to take risks and try new things.

A woman's life is positively impacted when she discovers that it's okay to be competitive—that whatever it is she wants, other people are likely to want it also—and that's just fine.

The Women's Way model was new and so were the challenges to make it work. The agencies signed on and agreed that the coalition would solicit individuals and businesses on their behalf—thus giving up their right to approach donors in those categories. They retained the right to seek grants and contracts from foundation and government sources, and Women's Way would stay away from those funders unless an exception was granted.

The structure of the board of directors was that each member agency had two seats on the Board and the agency directors had majority control. There was an equal number, minus one, of community representatives. A lively debate about including men on the board resulted in the addition of two wonderful men, both of whom played important roles in Women's Way's early success.

As chair of the fundraising campaign, I faced a new learning curve. I had participated in a number of fundraising events but never asked anyone directly for a contribution. The need to build a corporate funding base was especially daunting.

We found almost immediately that soliciting the business prospects was somewhat circular. We kept ending up where we started because United Way had not only established a beachhead, but had occupied the entire territory.

It wasn't that all the doors were closed. In many places the firms were cordial and some even listened to our story and sympathized with what we were doing. A few made modest gifts, which I came to think of as "throwing us a bone."

The no's were not a surprise. United Way had been around for decades. It was part of the landscape of community giving. We were the new kid on the block and, more significantly, we represented issues that were perceived as out of the mainstream.

My first corporate visit was to my former boss, Bill Grala, at Smith Kline and French. One of our two male board members went with me, and we sat across the desk from Bill and made our case. I'll always recall that Bill told me I was the first woman who had ever asked him for a direct contribution to an organization. He committed $2,500, one of our first, and largest, corporate gifts.

I learned quickly that once we were on a company's giving list, it was reasonable to expect annual contributions. That was true with Smith Kline until a few years later when I made my regular appeal and received an angry response. It turned out that one of our member agencies, Women Organized Against Rape, was participating in a demonstration boycotting one of Smith Kline's products, outside the company's headquarters! This was a painful lesson in the balancing act between representing organizations advocating changes in the treatment of women and seeking business support.

Early on, we considered steering clear of the corporate market, thinking perhaps we could just go after individuals. We found that many of them, especially working women, already had their giving tied up in payroll deductions with their employers expecting their pledges to go to the United Way.

The United Way system was enviable. Chaired by business leaders who convinced their peers to run their own internal pledge drives, there was an element of competition as companies added up the totals for employee giving and the business entity matched or doubled the amount in a corporate gift.

That deck was stacked against us. It was very difficult to secure corporate donations and next to impossible to get through to individual employees.

Nevertheless, we were committed to getting our story across to business officials. I knew some of them personally, and I felt they could be swayed to, at the very least, offer us some help. We were aware of the reality that corporate checks are hard to get, but once you get them, they don't bounce.

Sometimes companies will give because they believe in what you're doing without asking for any special credit. Other times, understandably, they give out of self-interest, especially when their marketing goals intersect with the charity's constituency. They want their buying public to know that citizenship in the community is part of their philosophy.

One of the first things I did when I took over as executive director in December of 1980 was to create an Advisory Council for Women's Way. Two business leaders initially signed on—a bank president and the head of a major accounting firm—then the head of an advertising agency and several prominent women who understood what we were trying to do. At the first meeting of the advisors, I asked for specific help including in-kind contributions. We left the meeting with the ad agency's commitment to provide pro bono creative materials and soon we had our first corporate fundraising brochure. I knew immediately that we were on to something.

At Women's Way, we kept reminding ourselves that we were unique and our approach hadn't been tried before. We were continually creating and recreating a new model, and women's agencies in other cities began to contact us for help. This was an inspiration for us, and we worked with several newly formed coalitions around the country.

I thought about the initiative a century earlier by two sisters, Victoria Woodhull and Tennessee Claflin. In 1870, they founded the first female-run brokerage company in America.

They did not do it alone. They persuaded the wealthy Cornelius Vanderbilt to support their aspirations with capital. Woodhull, Claflin & Co. became an instant success on Wall Street, so much so that Victoria Woodhull became the first woman presidential candidate in American history when she was nominated by the Equal Rights Party in 1872. Someone named Ulysses S. Grant would win reelection that year, but with women's right to vote still a half century away, Victoria Woodhull had made a statement.

Just as she had sought out Vanderbilt's help one hundred years earlier, we began to seek out corporate allies for Women's Way. We went after the market with zeal. Often turned away and frequently confronted with opposition, we plugged away, trying to convince companies of the importance of having their names associated with programs that supported women.

Most of the contributions managers were men, because most of the leadership jobs in business were held by men. However, as we began to recognize that most of them had wives and daughters at home, we started asking, "What kind of opportunity do you want your daughter to have when she grows up?" This approach was often successful.

We worked hard to get prominent, well-known companies on our roster of donors because that made it easier for others to follow. We were still being branded, incorrectly, as a single issue entity which focused primarily on reproductive rights. Not all companies were ready to withstand possible criticism by stepping forward to help us. Instead, many wanted to play it safe, to give where everyone else gives.

Progress was slow, but we were building a base of corporate support and, more importantly, of individual donations. Most of the latter were in the form of small checks, but a few wealthy donors, including some with family foundations, were writing larger checks. Our annual allocations to the members were gradually increasing and we were developing the important relationships which are so critical to successful fundraising.

When women encounter barriers in fundraising, we need to understand that such obstacles are part of the territory. We have to figure out how to get over them, around them or through them, and know that rejection is not personal.

A successful fundraiser must be an excellent communicator—through writing, speaking, listening, and "being."

Writing
You must be able to prepare a proposal that is clear, concise, correct, and complete. The words should not be too large to pronounce or too small to read in print. You need to make your proposal specific—a project or initiative that has a scheduled beginning date and an outcome with appeal.

Speaking

You must have the ability to clearly articulate your cause in front of individuals or boards. This is the "gather, package and deliver" stage. You'll want to convey, with confidence, that you believe this is just the right matchup for their charitable instincts. Remember, your competition includes all of the organizations that have been there before you. Prepare by thinking through in advance every question which might be asked. I operate on the theory that anything, to be perfectly spontaneous, must be carefully rehearsed.

Planned Listening

Learn everything you can about the person and company you're meeting with. Understand what they care about, their company mission and products, their hobbies, where they went to school, and what they like to talk about. Then be sure to listen carefully. Never be presumptuous about what interests them and what they may be passionate about.

Being

This refers to your "presence," how you carry yourself—your being involved, being concerned, being interested. Remember that it behooves you to be as interested in them as you want them to be in you. Communication by "being" is intangible, but it's an intangible you should not leave home without.

There are a few items which will be useful in your corporate fundraising tool kit. You'll need the business section of the newspaper because you're going to read it every day of your nonprofit life in order to find out which companies are doing well and which companies are struggling. You should also stock up on some nice note cards or, if you prefer e-mail, you can use that method of communication to send messages of congratulations or encouragement to companies you've been contacting. Keep in touch. Do not limit your contact to your annual request for funds. Instead, distinguish yourself by keeping in touch periodically.

At Women's Way we were determined not to be anyone's echo. We were getting some headlines. Our annual dinner was escalating to "banquet" status, enough so that we had to seek larger sites.

We became a magnet for strong women and for many more who wanted to be. Often at meetings, I looked at our gallant group of warriors—unpaid and underpaid—and I thought of writer Cynthia Heimel's advice—"There is a microscopically thin line between being brilliantly creative and acting like the most gigantic idiot on earth. So what the hell, leap!"

Motivated by circumstance, propelled by possibilities, we had leaped. The question remained, where would we land?

CHAPTER 11

Connections and Persistence—
Is There a Better Pair of Partners?

When the makers of the film classic *Wizard of Oz* finished the movie in 1939, they were concerned that it was too long and too sluggish in places. So before releasing it for previews at California theatres, they saved a few minutes by editing out a song sequence. After the preview, theatre owners complained that the movie was too short and people weren't getting their money's worth. Reluctantly, the song was put back in, to pad out the time. The song was "Somewhere over the Rainbow," which figures to last forever as the signature tune of the picture, of Judy Garland's career, and as an expression of hope. Rainbows were a good metaphor at Philadelphia's Women's Way. We knew that if we wanted to see a rainbow, we had to put up with the rain. We found out that in a downpour, it helps to link up with someone who has an umbrella.

The headline read UNITED WAY OBLIGES CHURCH, REBUFFS FEMINISTS.

This article—on the *Philadelphia Inquirer's* front page—proved to be pivotal in the Women's Way attempt to gain access to the United Way's workplace giving campaign.

The story quoted from a letter sent by the United Way president to Women's Way leaders denying Women's Way's request to enter into a partnership with United Way. It said, "Women's Way's insistence on including agencies and services that contravene the United Way's agreement with the Catholic Archdiocese make it unacceptable for funding."

The letter was a follow-up to a meeting of several Women's Way Board members, including me, with the United Way executive committee. We had requested the meeting to propose a collaborative relationship in which Women's Way would be eligible to receive contributions through the United Way campaign.

The story set off an enormous uproar in the Philadelphia region and made the national news. The problem was that most United Way supporters were unaware that there was an agreement with the Archdiocese that was influencing allocations of charitable contributions in what was supposed to be a community wide campaign.

As letters to the newspaper poured in, donors cancelled their United Way pledges and Women's Way quickly became a high-profile organization. The United Way's response was swift. They established a "committee on controversy," and just weeks later, the United Way had changed its course and created a new Donor Option Program to allow contributors to designate their gifts to nonprofit organizations outside the United Way, like Women's Way. The door to access was opening.

Hundreds, eventually thousands, of area nonprofits benefitted from this change in policy, and contrary to the arguments of United Way's advocates, overall giving increased as choices increased. During the first year of the Donor Option Program, Women's Way received $100,000 in designated contributions, second only to Catholic Charities.

Although there were many guardians of the status quo who were angry with Women's Way—and with me personally, as I became first the public relations director and then the executive director during that year—I persisted in championing donor choice. In what was a good strategic move by United Way, I was invited to serve on, and later chair, the Donor Option Implementation Committee to ensure that the program was administered efficiently and fairly.

It was a time of little mutual trust and a lot of negative feelings.

I hadn't counted on my husband paying a price for my growing public visibility. He was actually turned down for membership in a prestigious golf club because of it. He was told by the man who had proposed him as a member, "It's not because of you—it's your wife." Paul was furious and quickly wrote a check to Women's Way to help in the fight against discrimination. Nor was I prepared for the criticism I was getting from some business leaders and members of my church because I had challenged the United Way.

One more time I was able to call upon the long-ago messages of my father. He had made it clear to me that if you wanted to change something, it was important to stock up on two characteristics—being persistent and finding a way to connect with people who could help.

Persistence and connections—they usually come in that order. The more you have of the second, the less you need of the first.

Seeking change in long-established attitudes and institutions is never easy.

I recalled again that national meeting of Junior League chapters in Kansas City where I advocated the Association's endorsement of the Equal Rights Amendment's ratification. What I had run into then was a vivid illustration that some women prefer to have what they perceive as "special status" and they don't intend to give it up.

I saw the Equal Rights Amendment as an opportunity to improve the lives of all women. I believed that the majority of the seven hundred women assembled in Kansas City would see it that way too.

One surprising aspect of that conference was the discovery that there were eleven women delegates from across the United States who had attended my small college in Virginia, and several of them were from my class.

When the debate over ratification of the ERA came up on the agenda, I took a strong stand, advocating that a potentially powerful women's organization of over one hundred thousand members nationwide could be very persuasive in influencing state legislatures that had not yet voted on the issue.

Without intending to—or maybe I did—I became a leader of the pro-ratification forces at the conference.

Coincidentally, one of my former classmates was a key leader of those who felt the association should stay out of this controversy. When I asked her why she opposed the ERA, she replied, "Because I like being on a pedestal."

That was another lesson learned for me.

Some women, artificially spoiled by circumstances, prefer to turn away from the plight of so many of their sisters who have been shortchanged by an imbalance in human rights. It's that very philosophy of "I've got mine" that makes some women abandon the "DHAs" of others—D as in dreams, H as in hopes, A as in aspirations. I have never been able to do that.

Just as Women's Way had to challenge the inequities of a community fundraising campaign and try and change it for the better, I believe that women everywhere need to challenge unfair practices in business, politics, and all other areas of human endeavor.

It is not difficult to identify the obstacles women face in our social environment. We can compile an impressive list of things that are blocking our way.

What is difficult is admitting that a large part of what slows us down is internal. It's our own reluctance to make the commitment, separately and together, to dismantle external barriers.

When we acknowledge our own hesitation to stand up and speak out about our beliefs—that's when we become the "somebody" in that familiar phrase, "Somebody ought to do something!"

Sometimes when we run into a wall, we have to beat on it until it becomes a door. That's persistence.

Its companion, which may lead to a shortcut, is the ability to "connect." Men had a two-century head start in this race.

"Connecting" is what moves the ball ahead.

"Connecting" is why people have lunch together. For a long time women have limited lunch time to a food experience, using any extra moments to do errands or check on child care. Men, on the other hand, often use lunch to get one step closer to a promotion or a positive business deal.

That's why so many men play golf. It's why they hold those football huddles at cocktail parties, and why business cards were invented.

"Connecting" is about letters of recommendation, trading favors, opening doors, and opening minds previously closed to us.

In watching superachievers over the years, I've arrived at the conclusion that great women aren't great all the time. They couldn't be. It would exhaust them just being great. Greatness results from what you do and how you do it in those few minutes each day that are available to exercise greatness.

Billie Jean King did not wake up as a great tennis player one day. It was the way she used her hours every day that filled her shelves with world class championship trophies.

Sally Ride did not become a great astronaut overnight. It was her determination to use her time for preparation in such a way that when her trip into space had to be earned in a competition with many male astronauts, the greatness of her commitment won out.

Before I became familiar with the Unsinkable Molly Brown, I already knew about the Undefeatable Ernesta Ballard, who was both a lady and a legend. I owe her the Sunday Breakfast Club chapter of my life, among many other things.

Philadelphia's Sunday Breakfast Club started in 1933. It was an informal alliance of businessmen active in the Chamber of Commerce who would meet once a month to talk about mutual interests and civic concerns. With the nation sandwiched between two World Wars, in the midst of a devastating depression, and wondering what this upstart President Franklin D. Roosevelt would be like, there was no shortage of table conversation.

The meetings, which developed into monthly dinners on Wednesday nights, were held at the magnificent post-Civil War building which housed the all-male, very Republican Union League of Philadelphia.

Nearly fifty years after the club's founding, Ernesta Ballard was the first woman admitted to the Sunday Breakfast Club. She was then president of the Pennsylvania Horticultural Society, member of a prominent family, and married to one of Philadelphia's leading attorneys. She was also a passionate feminist, active in the National Organization for Women (NOW), and a cofounder of Women's Way.

Ernesta nominated me for membership in this somewhat mysterious club, and when she called to tell me I should accept the invitation, I reluctantly said, "I'll do it for Women's Way." She replied, "You must do it for women." At that time, there were fewer than a half-dozen women in the club's membership of more than three hundred, and Ernesta managed to get three of us admitted.

I should have been more curious that an outfit called the Sunday Breakfast Club actually met on Wednesday nights for dinner. I never really asked why, because from the very first session I attended, I could sense this was what "connecting" really meant. The Lincoln Ballroom was filled with leaders, and I recognized that this was a place to build important alliances.

My early adventures in the Sunday Breakfast Club led me into another unanticipated controversy.

While the club had opened its membership to women, the Union League, where we held our meetings, had not. In the early 1980s, some progressive men in the League—which had, by that time, admitted a few African American men and some Democrats—initiated a referendum among the membership to open the doors to women. The "door-opening" metaphor is appropriate since women had been required to enter the building through the lower level doors, not the main entrance.

A large turnout of Union League members weighed in on that referendum and, astonishingly to me, the majority voted to uphold the ban. I decided to take action.

I contacted the handful of women who were members of the Sunday Breakfast Club—all leaders in the community—and asked them to join me in petitioning the club to move its meetings out of the Union League. I did not want to attend events there nor did I want my club dues subsidizing a discriminatory institution. All but one of my women colleagues agreed.

A group of us met with the Club's all-male Steering Committee and appealed to their sense of fairness. We were successful in getting the organization to hold its meetings at another location. That move, among many others, hurt the Union League financially and ultimately led to the admission of women members a few years later. The Sunday Breakfast Club resumed its meetings there after that.

As with the United Way confrontation, my leadership role in this controversy cost me personally, especially after a story appeared in the *Philadelphia Inquirer*. Some of the male business leaders stopped speaking to me, and I felt generally unwelcome at Sunday Breakfast Club meetings for a while. However, I decided to "tough it out," and the negative feelings subsided.

Over the years, many friendships resulted from my club membership. Eventually, I was nominated to be chair of the steering committee, and I was in a position to open doors to more young people, more women, and more people of color.

"Connecting" has three rules.

Rule No. 1: At each event you attend, decide who you would like to meet and seek them out. To hope you'll wind up seated next to the "right people" is leaving too much to chance. "Connecting" is a contact sport. Be ready to make the first move.

Rule No. 2: Follow up with the people you want to stay in touch with. When people in "connecting" crowds promise that they'll call you, don't wait for them to make the next move. Barack Obama started out the first decade of the twentieth century by losing an unnoticed congressional primary in Illinois. He ended it as president of the United States. In between, he connected.

Rule No. 3: Ask for what you want. Women need to do a better job professionally of getting to the point. Most executives, particularly those in business, are comfortable solving problems and addressing requests. Be specific about what you'd like from the person you're talking to, and you have a much better chance at the desired outcome.

Early on, I discovered the "wish list" approach to soliciting corporate support.

Tipped off in advance of a meeting with a business official, I went in with a written "wish list" of ten specific Women's Way projects that needed funding. It was a "menu" of items that a company could choose from. Choosing to do nothing was *not* on the list.

By the time our tenth year arrived at Women's Way, we felt confident in our approach, in our growth, and in our results. Still something was missing. Then from out of nowhere, we found it.

CHAPTER 12

What Can We Learn from Women's History?

Our annual Women's Way event was celebrating its tenth Anniversary. It had been growing every year, but with that many energetic and enthusiastic women and men in the room, we needed something special to rally their resolve, to get them on their feet, cheering. We needed something dramatic to underscore our purpose, something of our own. We found the exclamation point in a song written on the other side of the ocean nearly a century earlier.

Lucretia Coffin Mott was born on Nantucket.

She grew up on that rugged island, far off the coast of Massachusetts, during its whaling era at the end of the eighteenth century and the early nineteenth century. Women living on Nantucket at that time had to be independent and in charge because men were off on whaling boats for months at a time, if they survived to come back at all.

Born in 1793, just a half dozen years after the U.S. Constitution was written, Lucretia Coffin attended a boarding school in Poughkeepsie, New York, where her performance was so admired that she made the transition from student to faculty member upon graduation.

Her first paycheck ignited her life's work. She found that women teachers received less than half the compensation their male counterparts did for the same work. The explanation that "men needed more money because they had more responsibilities" seemed weak to her. Other women teachers didn't like the disparity either, but they only whispered about it, never raising their voices.

Lucretia Coffin married James Mott, but did not embrace the role of a "normal" housewife. Stung by the mixed message of a new nation bragging about freedom as its cornerstone while permitting deprivation of liberty for many, she went on what we would now call the "lecture circuit," speaking out in opposition to slavery and the second-class status of women.

After moving to Philadelphia, she became president of the Philadelphia Female Antislavery Society. The title describes how she invested most of her eighty-seven years. She endured death threats for her position against slavery, and then found her problems doubled when she traveled to London to participate in a world antislavery conference and was turned away at the door because she was female.

It was Lucretia Mott who joined Elizabeth Stanton in calling for the 1848 Seneca Falls convention in New York, from which was issued the "Declaration of Sentiments" demanding equality before the law for women.

Throughout her life, often in front of hostile audiences, she spoke out for women's rights, pursuing her career right up until a few months before her death in 1880.

So, in the 1970s, when Women's Way made a decision to present an annual award to an outstanding woman at our fundraising dinner, there was almost no debate about who to name it for. We chose Lucretia Mott because she was a pioneer for women's rights and because she had the courage to stand up to resistance and hostility—two conditions still evident nearly a century after her death. We learned about her through her biographer, Women's Way board member Margaret Bacon.

The Lucretia Mott Award helped build immediate credibility when it was accepted in its first year by Coretta Scott King. In the second year, 1979, an even larger audience came to see Joan Ganz Cooney, creator of Sesame Street, accept the award. A few years later, award recipient Gloria Steinem's appearance drew 750 attendees, and after that the event had to be moved to the largest hotel ballroom in Philadelphia.

We began to regard the dinner as both a significant fundraising opportunity and also a rallying call for women who wanted to show their solidarity in protesting the unfair rules that governed many aspects of their lives.

As the tenth Anniversary Dinner approached, we knew we needed something to make the evening special. We found it, and that spring evening in 1987 became a turning point for Women's Way and for the two thousand women and men who participated.

Most individuals and organizations can point to pivotal events in their histories. The Civil Rights momentum was greatly accelerated by the action of Rosa Parks sitting down on a bus in 1955, and by a speech eight years later in Washington by Martin Luther King Jr. In 1991, the verbal attacks on Anita Hill at a Senate hearing sparked the consciousness of women throughout America.

On a personal level, sometimes it's a tragedy that adds even more determination to what one wants to do with his/her life. That's what happened to me in 1986 with my brother's sudden death at the age of forty-three.

I have never asked exactly where Po was when the car hit him. "Po" was short for Porter, and that was what I called him throughout his life. I do know that he had gone out to look for his neighbor's dog late on a Friday evening in July and was crossing the main road near his Virginia Beach home.

I was asleep in my suburban Philadelphia home the next morning when I heard someone banging on the front door. It was the local police telling me that my phone was out of order and to call my brother's number. To my surprise, my father answered and handed the phone to my mother. My shock at the news was profound and lasting.

I thought of Po's wife and his two children. I thought of all that can be lost in an instant, for he was a son, a husband, a father, and a brother. His death was a loss for so many so suddenly. Most of all Po lost his life and his opportunity to achieve goals he had not yet even dreamed.

Dealing with unfair circumstances was part of the life I had chosen for myself, but this was a new kind of challenge to me. It became a wake-up call to the fragility of life and the realization that we can't take our time on earth for granted.

With Po's death, I put a new value on committing every moment I could find to make my own life more useful. In that way, my brother's death inspired me. I did not want to waste a single day or opportunity to make a difference. Looking at the lives of women I had admired through history, I realized how intelligently they had used their time to bring changes to the world.

Lorraine Hansberry was allotted thirty-five years on this planet, but she used them to arouse the social conscience of America through her work on behalf of "forgotten people." Her play, *A Raisin in the Sun*, was the first such production by an African American woman to appear on Broadway. When it opened at the Ethel Barrymore Theatre and won the New York Drama Critic's Circle award for best play of 1959, Lorraine Hansberry was twenty-nine.

Carol Weiss King lived fifty-seven years. She became a lawyer in 1920, and unable to find a job with a law firm, she rented an office to start a career of defending clients others had abandoned. She was often branded as a "commie" for defending and defining the rights of aliens, and would go on to enlighten and influence a generation of attorneys on the strategy and tactics of constitutional litigation.

Anna Mary Moses lived 101 years, until 1961. She left home at twelve to work as a hired girl. At twenty-seven, she married a farmer and settled down in Virginia to raise ten children. After her husband's death, at a farm in New York, she began painting to "pass the time." In the years ahead, her first work, displayed in a drug store, led to a permanent collection housed at the Metropolitan Museum of Art in New York. Ignored by art critics, but loved by the public, Grandma Moses painted well into her midnineties.

One lived thirty-five years, another fifty-seven, another 101. What they had in common was a belief in using their time, whatever its limits, and their talent, whatever its boundaries, to the fullest extent. I wanted to do that myself, and I also wanted to convey the message of "be-your-own-hero" to our Women's Way audience.

Our tenth Anniversary Dinner was the ideal place to do this.

That's when the idea of a closing visual surfaced. Perhaps we could give everyone a lift by showing images of prominent, courageous women—some of them famous, some of them less known, but all of them a vivid patch on a quilt of the tragedies and triumphs of women trying to right what was wrong.

The challenge was how to put up hundreds of old and not-so-old photographs on the screen and bring them to life in such a way that it would engage our audience. We were eager to have Women's Way supporters loosen up their checkbooks and get into a can't-wait-to-come-back-next-time frame of mind.

Dick Jackman, the most creative person I have ever known, and Women's Way's most generous corporate supporter at Sunoco, came up with the concept that the right music, carefully fitted to the photos, might create such a reaction. And that's when Sir Edward Elgar came into my life.

Actually, I had heard his most famous musical piece often in the past, but didn't know he was the composer who had taken the title for his music from Act 3, Scene 3 of Shakespeare's *Othello*.

I listened to a rendition of "Pomp and Circumstance," the music almost totally associated with graduation ceremonies. My immediate reaction was to laugh. Visions of caps and gowns danced freely in front of me. Then I closed my eyes and imagined impressive photos of women—each picture especially timed to the music. What I envisioned led me to say, "Let's give it a try."

Modern video techniques were still in the future. In order to achieve the motion and emotion that we wanted, multiple slide projectors and elaborate synchronization were required. It was going to be a pass/fail in front of two thousand people.

The first time I saw a rough cut of the presentation, I took along a couple of my staff members to the screening room. The pictures of Eleanor Roosevelt, Amelia Earhart, Jackie Kennedy, Rosa Parks, Olympic heroes, marchers for women's rights, girls, and women of all ages—all of this was backdropped by music so powerful it became a costar. Then a thundering finish—with a rapid review of the photos, and a sudden stop. All in a little over three minutes.

As the lights came on in the screening room, I noticed my staff members wiping the tears from their eyes. It was difficult for me to see them. My own tears were getting in the way. What we had just seen in less than four minutes was a whole drama of history and human valor.

How would a large crowd react? We had only one chance. We didn't have long to wait for our answer. When the faces hit the screen and the music hit all the notes, the cheers started spontaneously. Then the shouts. Then people were on their feet cheering.

The show became an instant success—and an instant tradition which has been updated for showing every year for over twenty years. Enriched by technology and new breakthroughs for women, it becomes more powerful each year. The audience expects it and waits for it. It belongs to them, and they belong to what it means.

It really says, "How badly do you want what life can be?" This message of inspiration is important to the people who have struggled daily for recognition and equality. Sometimes that inspiration needs to be internalized, particularly in light of a possibility we hadn't considered—that one of women's toughest foes may be ourselves.

CHAPTER 13

Are Women Leaders Different from Men?

The movie *Thelma and Louise* stars Susan Sarandon and Geena Davis. It is a buddy film, almost a female version of *Butch Cassidy and the Sundance Kid*, with Paul Newman and Robert Redford. It's about two women trapped in dismal lives complicated by their own choices. They discover the freedom they have been denied on a weekend that brings them elation, then tragedy. Along the way Thelma complains about a bad husband and a sheltered life. Louise responds, "You get what you settle for."

It's strange that we still have a "power gap" between men and women. It shouldn't exist by all the laws of mathematics.

Women constitute a majority of the population of America, but you wouldn't know that by counting heads in Congress, where the percentage of women is still less than one in five.

Women own more than half the corporate stock in the U.S., but you can't tell by the boards of directors of Fortune 500 companies, where the small numbers of women conjure up the word "tokenism."

By any measurement women's progress is too slow. Perhaps it's because what's at stake is power. Men who have it work hard to protect it. Women, who may define it differently, would like more.

One condition is certain. Our "power failures" are not going to be solved by men.

There is nothing in our history to encourage the feeling that rescue is on the way and that men will be leading the charge. That's a train that just isn't going to arrive, no matter how hopefully we wait at the station.

Public attitudes for generations were shaped to assign labels of leadership pretty much to "men only." Women generally did the work men did not want to do.

The woman as "boss" was rare as recently as the 1980s. A big part of the problem was at the workplace entry point—women often couldn't get hired in managerial jobs because of perceived inadequate experience. Of course, what wasn't taken into consideration was the multiple-managing they were doing in a household. Translating home and community experience into marketable skills is a challenge we have faced for years.

At Women's Way, we developed and appreciated our managers. We demonstrated that women working together toward a common goal can achieve great things, that power can be shared, and that leadership can be nonhierarchical.

A few years later and several thousand miles away, I found a refreshing endorsement of my belief that leadership—male or female—is about setting the agenda, developing creative ideas, solving problems, and empowering others.

It was in October of 1993 at the conclusion of a year of travel and lectures following my run for the U.S. Senate. I was delivering the keynote address at an International Management Symposium for women in Zurich, Switzerland.

My speech dealt with the transition from emotional commitment to specific action, and I hit hard on the value of leadership that empowers others—particularly women, because we are the ones without the power.

As I left the podium, a man I had never seen came bounding down the aisle toward me. He gave me an energetic hug and introduced himself as Ben Zander, conductor of the Boston Philharmonic Orchestra. His message to me was that my view of leadership and its responsibilities was consistent with his.

That evening when he had the floor, he talked to the audience about a conductor's duty. "In an orchestra," Zander said, "the conductor never makes a sound."

Leadership is sometimes a gift, often an art and always a discipline. For too long, women have stifled the very characteristics that discipline requires, characteristics we have in abundance. Perhaps some shy away from seeking positions of power because of the heat that goes with it, but as Ben Zander made clear to me, "If you're going to lead the orchestra, you have to turn your back to the crowd."

If women are going to act like the majority we are, some commitments to action will be necessary. I created a set of commitments for myself when I acknowledged my life's work of improving the status of women in our society.

Writing a letter to the editor in our head when we read something which is unfair, infuriating or positive—but failing to send it—doesn't change a thing. We need to act on our anger and express our appreciation.

Here is my six-part pledge, written many years ago:

1. *Wherever women or our issues are dismissed, distorted, or discounted, respond with speed and substance to correct the circumstance.*
2. *Wherever women are denied fair access to leadership opportunities, immediately challenge those exclusions.*
3. *Wherever women are shortchanged economically, protest this inequity promptly, visibly, and vocally.*
4. *Wherever women are treated unfairly by the media, speak out with purpose to correct the situation.*
5. *Wherever women are judged by our gender instead of our genius, challenge vigorously all farms of such abuse.*
6. *Wherever women are boosted by positive actions taken to enhance our progress, publicly applaud those efforts.*

Practice these actions and good things happen. Ignore them and live by Louise's law—"You get what you settle for."

When these six principles are adopted by someone, a sense of change begins to happen in her life. When they are embraced by numbers of women, the change becomes more widespread.

Class action lawsuits to correct damage done by years of unfair practices often earn headlines for the amount of money won by the plaintiffs and their lawyers, but the real difference comes in the policies that are changed because of the legal action. Sometimes one voice of protest is the same as the tree falling in the forest when no one is around to hear it, but put many voices together and support them with strong leadership to follow through on the task, and that voice becomes loud enough to change practices that have stood for centuries.

Sometimes there are behavior patterns that cause women to be our own worst enemies in effecting change.

One is complacency. The throw-up-your-hands concession of "that's just the way things are and I'm too busy to get involved." That excuse makes us unable, or unwilling, to see that it *isn't* the way things have to be.

The other issue that slows the pace of change for women is the tendency to abandon our individuality and personal strengths in order to be accepted by the status quo. To be so anxious to secure power that we go along with the very practices that made us resent those who perpetuated them undermines opportunities for all of us.

In the long debate over gender roles, men and women have different advantages.

Men generally have a physical advantage in terms of strength. In most cases, they can run faster, win a tug-of-war and handle heavier weights.

What's the edge for women? I believe it's the built-in instinct for understanding the human experience. When we give that up just to achieve power, we are forfeiting the opportunity to stimulate the change we're seeking.

If the rules are wrong, our focus must be on how to make them right. If the system of fairness-for-all is corrupt, our energy must be devoted to correcting that system.

Some of my most interesting debates with men revolve around my conviction that, as a rule, women are more honest than men.

I didn't think about the subject so much when I was working to establish a reliable funding source for women's agencies, though I did question the integrity of a charitable contribution system that screened women out. My observations on the male/female approach to actual truth-telling really came to the surface during my experience with politics.

One of the painful lessons of political campaigns is the discovery that there are simply no enforceable standards of conduct for candidates. False charges can be made without accountability. People who are hungry for power will say almost anything! I found it shocking and disappointing that some people could look me in the eye and simply lie.

We know women didn't invent this, because politics was a going concern long before women were even permitted to be on its fringes.

In my 1992 campaign, we came up with the slogan, "Fight Truth Decay."

Throughout history, in almost every line of endeavor, women have been measured differently from men and are frequently held to a higher standard. I found this double standard frustrating and discouraging as I waged my high-profile political battle.

Even before that experience, in watching Women's Way grow in the '80s and as it became clear that women were beginning to understand the benefits of working together, I spoke out urging the coalition to walk the high ground, to stand firm on our principles, not to compromise our integrity.

What we were realizing as we moved from the '80s to the '90s was that second-class treatment, job discrimination, and sexual harassment could no longer be tolerated. One of the women saying it softly, but in a voice heard throughout the nation, was speaking from a Senate hearing room in Washington. Her name was Anita Hill. I listened carefully.

CHAPTER 14

When Will We Cheer for Overdogs?

Madeleine Albright, U.S. Secretary of State in the 1990s, said it: "Public service is the most rewarding kind of life you can have . . . but it exposes you to a lot of criticism and you have to develop a thick skin. As a woman, you have to remember who you are and not try to be a man, to remember that the various capabilities that women have of multitasking and being empathetic will serve you very well." She also said, "There's a special place in hell for women who don't help each other."

In 1991 I didn't know Senator Arlen Specter well.

I knew his wife, Joan Specter, who was a member of the Women's Way advisory council. She was also a Philadelphia City Councilwoman, and in late September, she was the focus of a $250-a-head fundraiser that Paul and I attended.

Although I had no thought of it in my mind at the time, in one hundred days I would make a decision to compete for her husband's job. With politics in my bloodline, I had considered running for Congress when my representative had given up his seat to challenge Arlen Specter several years earlier. But it was the wrong time then, personally and professionally, and I hadn't given it much thought since.

Arlen Specter had received national attention in the 1960s as the author of the controversial "single-bullet theory" in the investigation of John F. Kennedy's assassination. His political career had taken him from District Attorney in Philadelphia to the U.S. Senate. By 1991 he had achieved significant seniority in the Senate and was a member of the powerful Senate Judiciary Committee.

At the September fundraiser for his wife, I chatted with Specter about President Bush's nomination of Clarence Thomas to the Supreme Court. Thomas' strict antichoice position on women's reproductive rights was one I strongly differed with, and I knew Specter's view was similar to mine. He changed the subject to ask if I would consider recruiting Democratic women to switch parties and vote for him in his primary race the following April against a Pennsylvania State Senator who vigorously opposed abortion rights.

Any chance of that happening vanished two weeks later when Specter led the televised questioning of witness Anita Hill, who had worked with Clarence Thomas when he was Chairman of the Equal Employment Opportunity Commission.

I had never heard of Anita Hill, but there was no doubt that her explosive testimony about being sexually harassed on the job by Thomas changed a routine hearing into a national controversy.

In the middle of it was Arlen Specter, leading the attack on Hill's testimony. Specter questioned her motives, and he implied that she was lying about her relationship with Thomas. It was a classic case of the alleged victim being classified as the villain.

To me, his conduct was incomprehensible. It showed a decided lack of respect. In humiliating one woman, he was insulting all women, and it was clear that neither he, nor his committee colleagues "got it" with regard to sexual harassment. Part of my outrage came from my realization that just two weeks earlier he had asked me to persuade Democrats to jump parties and vote for him in the 1992 Republican primary. As I watched the hearings on TV, I went from disbelief to anger to fury.

What those fourteen all-white men grilling one African American woman couldn't seem to understand was that Anita Hill represented every woman who has ever been demeaned, dismissed, or sexually compromised by a man who had authority over her. Women understood this because it was about an imbalance of power we can relate to. Every woman who had ever tried to make progress in the workplace on her professional merits, but had been invited to supplement those credentials with personal favors, understood what Anita Hill was describing.

Anita Hill's testimony began on a Friday, and the hearing continued all weekend. On Monday, it was the talk of the office, the town, and the telephone lines.

At Women's Way, work practically came to a halt as the anger built, most of it directed at the U.S. Senator from Pennsylvania, Arlen Specter.

One of my Monday phone calls came from a columnist with the *Philadelphia Daily News*, who said, "Lynn, you have to run against Arlen Specter."

Strangely I didn't reject the idea.

Others called with the same suggestion, saying, "A woman has to challenge him."

I agreed with that.

My friends knew of my interest in politics, my childhood in a political family, and my summer jobs on Capitol Hill during high school. Plus, I had become known as "the somebody who does something." Responsibility was something I accepted and even reached for, only now the stakes were extremely high. We needed a woman to run for the U.S. Senate.

The timing was right for me. My children were away at college and law school. My work at Women's Way, though far from complete, was at a point where someone else could pick up the baton.

Still, it was a daunting decision to make and I didn't rush. There were other women around who were more qualified through their political experience. I checked with them to see if they were considering a run against Specter. None was ready to step forward.

Maybe part of their reluctance was created by the fact that a formidable field of Pennsylvania Democratic men were already clamoring for the nomination, including Lieutenant Governor Mark Singel, the odds-on favorite to win the Democratic nomination.

I talked to my friend, Senator Harris Wofford, who had been appointed to succeed Senator John Heinz after Heinz was killed in an April 1991 airplane collision and had won a special election that fall to keep the seat.

Harris suggested I call political consultant James Carville, who had helped him win the recent election. I met with Carville. He was just as he appeared on television, a political cowboy, but a no-nonsense communicator who did not sugarcoat the priorities.

Carville's first question to me was, "Do you have money?" I answered in the affirmative knowing that the gifts from my parents and grandfather had led to successful investments in the stock market.

In addition, raising funds was what I had been doing for a dozen years. I knew where the money was, and I wasn't afraid to ask for it.

I kept checking with people whose opinions I valued. What did my trusted pastor, Gene Bay, think? His first question, in response to mine, was "*What's your position on Israel?*" I wish I'd understood the significance of that question at the time. He also asked me if I thought it would be worth it to get my message out even if I didn't win. That, too, was a good question, and it was impossible to answer.

My family almost unanimously opposed the idea, except for my dog, who was neutral. My father, 88 years old at the time, tried to talk me out of it. He said, "Politics has changed. Washington is no place to be now." As a man who had gone through a dozen congressional campaigns, he knew how much turbulence was ahead of me, especially in a presidential election year. Later, after I had made my decision to run, he would say, "I'm not surprised. I've been expecting it."

And he sent me a check.

So did lots of other people. At a New Year's Day party in 1992, I tested the financial waters by asking five people to give $1,000 each to my campaign. They all said yes.

Even with this encouragement, I thought about all there was to lose. I could use up my savings, disrupt my family, ruin my marriage, and be out of a job. This time I wasn't running for office in the Junior League. I knew intuitively that once I crossed the line from my private life to a high-stakes public office pursuit, there would be no going back.

Most people could not see beyond the Anita Hill incident when looking for my motivation. However, I had many other reasons, nearly all of them related to the scarcity of women in high political office, a sort of enforced consignment of women to roles in society where our voices and choices could be easily ignored. There were only two women in the U.S. Senate at that time. As then-Senate candidate Dianne Feinstein said, "2 percent is okay for milk, but not for the U.S. Senate." I wanted to be in a position to influence priorities and allocate resources to issues I knew women care about.

Through it all, I remembered the pledge I had made following my brother's death five years earlier—to make every minute count in a life that had an unpredictable length.

I'm not a fan of delays and postponements. I shudder when I think of the times I have heard people tell women, "Your time will come."

To me, duty is not a calendar issue. It is not a seasonal thing. Vigilance on behalf of justice is a year-around job. I knew how I felt about sex discrimination and sexual harassment, for example. These behaviors are wrong on four counts.

They are wrong because . . .

They treat women as objects to be manipulated, exploited, or ignored, rather than as peers. They prevent women from being taken seriously and realizing our human potential.

Those who harass or discriminate would never tolerate such treatment of their wives or daughters.

They are against the law and against any reasonable standard of decency in human conduct.

The issue of sexism, or what some scholars call "implicit bias," is troubling because it is so deeply entrenched in our society—in the media, in established institutions and attitudes, and even among women who become convinced that they are less competent than men, or worse, that they deserve to be treated badly.

In researching the origins of gender inequality, I stopped at twenty-four centuries ago. Aristotle, a pretty big name in wisdom, is generally acclaimed for his worldly views, but even he had a narrow set of boundaries for women. He said, "The male is by nature superior, and the female inferior, and one rules, and the other is ruled. This principle, of necessity extends to all mankind."

When you start out twenty-four centuries behind, you know you have a long way to go to catch up.

Writer Molly Haskell calls the idea of women's inferiority a myth, saying, "It is a lie so deeply ingrained in our social behavior that merely to recognize it is to risk unraveling the entire fabric of civilization."

As I mulled over the prospect of running for political office, I thought about the pattern of patriarchy, how women grow up learning to submit to the control of others.

I had decided I would wait until New Year's Eve—until the last possible minute before the election year of 1992—to make my go/no-go decision. This was a self-imposed deadline because I simply couldn't keep postponing it.

Paul and I were in New York City with our longtime friends, Jan and Gene Kiley. The four of us usually welcomed in the New Year together, but this time we decided to make it special with an overnight stay.

When I told my friend Jan that day that I was thinking about running for the Senate, she was stunned. I even asked her not to mention it at dinner because Paul was pretty sure I was out of my mind for even toying with the idea.

As the clock was running out on the year and on my timetable, the four of us stopped at Fifth Avenue Presbyterian Church where a midnight service was underway.

I've always found that being in church removes the clutter from my mind. It worked again. I thought it out and prayed hard for guidance. And the answer came. I thought, *Yes I will do it. I'll take a leave from Women's Way. Perhaps I can do more good for the causes we care about by being a candidate.*

I met my deadline, made the decision to run, and greeted a new year that I could not have anticipated. I'm glad I decided to take on the challenge, because it's almost impossible in retrospect to imagine what my life would have been like if I'd spent that year differently.

A friend added a note of what I took for cheer after hearing about my decision: "This guarantees you will go to heaven, because by the time you get through this campaign, you will have been through hell."

CHAPTER 15

If Women Are Single-Issue Candidates, What Is the Issue?

Men make houses. Women make homes. A woman does not run for public office alone. She is accompanied everywhere by a constant companion named guilt. Tradition and nature have made woman the caregiver. She can have a successful husband, two bright children, the comfortable home, but not the full freedom to chase the unfulfilled ambition. After all, she has to keep the plants alive.

What a difference a gender makes!

Right up until the moment I announced my intention to run for the Democratic nomination for the U.S. Senate, I couldn't get rid of the warning I'd received that "running for political office was different for a woman."

I certainly wasn't the first woman to exercise her delayed citizenship by seeking success at the polls, but I may have been among the most unprepared for what was about to happen.

I was no stranger to political campaigns. I had watched my father as he conducted his vote-getting in Virginia, and handled occasional attacks from political opponents, during his more than two decades in Congress. He took a little heat on the campaign trail, but it was minor in volume and he hardly seemed to notice it, or so it appeared to me.

Of course, he had an advantage over me. He was a man. Men were expected to be politicians. Women, particularly those testing the campaign waters for the first time, had a difficult time being taken seriously. Even today, nearly a century after finally securing the right to vote, women candidates for high office remain somewhat of a novelty.

The "toughness" issue is always present for a woman candidate. Is she tough enough? Will she fall apart at the first sound of disagreement with her positions on key issues? Is her skin, which will also be judged on its complexion, thick enough to withstand wave after wave of false charges?

A political campaign is a battle of wills and personalities disguised as a contest of principles. Who has the will to stay with the battle? Who will do whatever it takes to win? I recalled the words of Adlai Stevenson, twice a candidate for U.S. President: "Anyone who will do the things it takes to win the office doesn't deserve to be president."

The essence of politics is power—the struggle to achieve it, the competition to maintain it, the temptation to abuse it.

Women have very little preparation for power struggles. Tradition, intentionally planned or accidentally achieved, has either put women on a pedestal, protected from the political fray, or kept them in powerless positions—economically and socially—where they have no hope of competing. Women of my generation were allowed to be spectators, but if we dared to try getting into the game, we found the door locked from the inside.

The image of the smoke-filled rooms where decisions were being made that would affect our lives and those of our children did not include one half of the population.

For the most part, a woman in the twentieth century had to be content with one political assignment—to stand by her man. Her job was to be the faithful wife, content to wave from the platform, to select the right dress for the swearing in, to smile for family photos, but to keep her opinions to herself.

The arrival, and subsequent dominance, of television as a political campaign reality created an additional burden for the stereotypical wife of a public figure. Without rehearsal, she had to be a silent sentry in the format that has become what I call the "scandal syndrome."

The pattern is familiar and predictable.

Rumors surface that the politician has had, is having, or is thinking about having, an intimate relationship with one or more women other than the one to whom he is married. The candidate vigorously denies the charge and flails his critics for gutter tactics in manufacturing such slander on his spotless character. Charges and countercharges are reported by assorted media representatives. At some point the accused can be counted on to rely on the phrase that it's "beneath his dignity" to respond further.

That is when the surprise video taken by an underpaid motel clerk surfaces. Or the recorded phone call, e-mail, or text message. Or the "other woman" herself, encouraged by the prospect of a tabloid fee, a possible book deal and a talk show appearance or two, suddenly speaks up.

Enter the scripted confess-all press conference by the candidate. And who is that standing just to his right, wearing the pale blue suit with the matching look on her face, playing her proper role in this public humiliation? The wife. With her "stand by her man" credentials barely able to mask her anger and embarrassment.

As more and more women indicated in the closing years of the twentieth century and the opening ones of the twenty-first, we began to feel we could do a better job in public office than was being done.

The men's rooms (only) in the U.S. Senate chambers began to get new signs.

What many women encountered was trouble—trouble getting access to campaign funds, trouble accepting the unwritten rules of political gamesmanship long ago established by the "good old boys," trouble making the case for the "experience" they had not had the opportunity to get, and trouble dealing with a different standard of treatment in media coverage and voters' ambivalent attitudes.

So before I decided on my strategy in 1992, I did some sober research of what had happened in 1984 to Geraldine Ferraro when she accomplished the historical breakthrough of becoming the vice presidential running mate of Walter Mondale.

I remember the excitement and anticipation among women all across America. Millions of women became involved in the political process. For the first time, many contributed time, emotional energy, and money—Ferraro actually raised more money than Mondale. At a rally I attended for her in Philadelphia, I recall vividly the optimistic fervor of the standing-room-only crowd.

Inspired by Ferraro's example, a record number of women ran for Congress. Most of them lost. Two years later it was far more difficult to convince women that they should sign up to wage political war.

What was it that happened to dampen their enthusiasm?

Geraldine Ferraro endured a withering campaign in which prime public issues were virtually ignored while the media and the opposition hammered away at sidebar subjects, mostly the activities of her husband.

Ferraro herself became the object of excessive public attack. Her personal life was put under a microscope. The media were relentless in criticizing her hair, her appearance, her voice, her family. Every action she had ever taken and every statement she had ever made were fair game.

That message went out to all women—there was a price to be paid for even trying to share power, and the price for many was too high.

As I thought about getting into the high profile Senate race in Pennsylvania, an excerpt from a column by Richard Cohen seemed to send me a warning. "The public stoning of Geraldine Ferraro," Cohen wrote, "goes on and on, and no one comes to her defense—not even her own kind."

If Ferraro, an established U.S. Congresswoman, could not rely on women to sustain their early enthusiasm and rally to her side, what were my chances as a political newcomer of building the winning base, even among women who felt as I did about the Anita Hill abuse?

I really didn't have to look at the national Ferraro picture to realize what I was up against. Judge Genevieve Blatt had won the Democratic Party nomination for the U.S. Senate in Pennsylvania back in 1964. I was to become only the second woman in our Commonwealth's history to win a major party nomination for the U.S. Senate—a statistic still valid in 2010.

Why had nearly three decades elapsed between Judge Blatt's candidacy and mine? I should have known there was a reason.

To this day I am fascinated by the parallel developments of campaigns conducted twenty-eight years apart. It was as if time stood still.

Judge Blatt won the Democratic primary on April 28, 1964, in an upset victory over the party-endorsed candidate. Even the day of the month was the same for both of *us*.

Genevieve Blatt's opponent in the fall election was a powerful Republican incumbent, the late Hugh Scott.

Up against a foe that would outspend her by a wide margin, she endured attacks on her character that consumed her campaign time defending herself against false charges. All of this was documented in a book entitled *Bigotry!* Unfortunately, I was unaware of that book until after my campaign.

It was "back to the future" in terms of the similarities between her campaign experience and mine. But even if I had foreseen the prospect of history repeating itself, this was a race I had to run. The stories of Blatt and Ferraro clearly communicated the old political fact that negative campaigning is mean-spirited, intellectually dishonest, and unfortunately, brutally effective.

I knew what I expected of myself.

I would be a champion and spokesperson for women, an advocate of social justice and individual liberty. I would speak out for people who had no voice in the political process. I wanted equal treatment for all before the courts, in the workplace, and in every other facet of American life.

One of my goals was to avoid making promises I couldn't keep. I was determined not to make deals for votes. I wanted all cards on the table, face up. Idealism? Of course, but what's wrong with that?

It was disappointing to discover how deeply entrenched the power structure was. Having guarded the status quo so vigilantly for decades, those men who held power were prepared to do whatever it took to protect it.

It's upsetting to see, even today when the public should know better, the challenges faced by women candidates for public office. What is a "woman's issue?" Does a stand for equal pay, family health, and good education for children somehow make a woman "soft" on matters such as national defense?

Hillary Clinton dispelled many of the stereotypes in her historic run for the presidency in 2008, clearly demonstrating women's interests and expertise in a wide range of subjects and rejecting traditional assumptions about women's roles.

The decision to run gave me a public platform for speaking out on issues large and not-so-large, but with it came formidable twin challenges—assembling a team and raising money. Taking on Arlen Specter was the goal, but there was the matter of winning the Democratic primary first, and the odds made me the longest of long shots.

I lined up a team of people I knew and with whom I was comfortable. Some had campaign experience and many did not, but they were energetic, loyal, capable and totally committed.

I went to Washington to explore money-raising options and met with Ellen Malcolm of Emily's List and the leaders of the Women's Campaign Fund and National Women's Political Caucus. I came away encouraged.

So far, every light was green. Then the pollster I had hired to check out my name recognition in the sixty-seven counties of Pennsylvania reported some statewide results. The poll said my name recognition among voters was one percent.

That meant that with only about ninety days left until the April 28 primary election, 99 percent of Pennsylvania voters had no idea who I was. We clearly had some work to do.

CHAPTER 16

Can We Handle the Loss of Privacy in a Run for Public Office?

I've always admired the high divers in the swimming competition of the Olympic games. They stand all alone on that stark platform high above the water knowing everybody is watching them and that they must perform brilliantly on the way down because unforgiving judges are ready to second-guess their every maneuver. They have a choice. They can retreat, climb back down that ladder, pack their gym bag, find a ride to the airport, and go home. Or they can step off that platform and do their best.

Politics is a lot like parenting.

You have to know when to be patient and when not to be. When to seek advice, and when to go with your own intuition. How to push—without being pushy.

Whether it's raising a child or running a campaign, when it's over, you'll always feel you could have done better. In the case of children, you will measure your success with the question, "How did they turn out?" In the case of politics, the question to be eventually answered is: "How did *you* turn out?"

The campaign team I recruited, nearly all of them women, had three characteristics in common. The first was that most had never been involved in a statewide campaign and many had no political experience at all on their resumes.

The second thing they shared was a commitment to women's progress and an intense dislike for what had happened to Anita Hill. Their anger, clearly directed toward Senator Arlen Specter, made them willing to be agents of change.

The third quality they each had in abundance was loyalty.

I have always valued loyalty, especially when it's combined with passion. Loyalty to the cause of justice has consistently been at the top of my "what's important" list. Loyalty need not be blind, and must not be artificial.

Truly loyal people will help you when you're hurting, will applaud you when you're doing things right—and will rein you in when you're doing something dumb.

In a way, our campaign team's ignorance of "the way things were done" and our inexperience in traditional political behavior would prove to be a strength. We weren't savvy enough to know that a candidate whom ninety-nine out of one hundred Pennsylvanians had never heard of could not possibly mount a campaign that would secure the Democratic nomination over a tested vote-getter.

Some of the women who had been with me through rough battles at Women's Way now stepped up with enthusiasm to a new challenge—how to win this primary election.

One of them touted the Yeakel glass as more than half full, saying, "There are advantages to being new. Those of us who haven't done this are not as burned out as some who have. Beyond that, when you sense that you're losing your rights, that keeps your motivation high."

There were many other women who came forward, some of them cautiously at first. All would be helpful.

In somewhat of a breakthrough that represented considerable courage, two women became the first elected officials to endorse my candidacy—Pennsylvania State Senator Allyson Schwartz and Philadelphia City Councilwoman Marian Tasco.

Recognizing the peculiar geography and population distribution of Pennsylvania, we orchestrated a three-stop announcement day—in Pittsburgh, Philadelphia, and Harrisburg. It was an overwhelming day, and I was semiterrified by all the media attention, realizing that, as I crossed the line from my private life to a public one, I could never go back entirely.

An event that made Allyson's and Marian's actions earn my bravery award occurred two days after that official announcement. That was when the Democratic State Committee met in Philadelphia to endorse candidates in the spring primary election.

I was fully aware that I wasn't going to win the support of the party establishment, but I set up a hospitality suite at their hotel in hopes of talking committee members into foregoing an endorsement, thus creating an open primary. Since there were five of us seeking the Democratic nomination for the U.S. Senate seat, it seemed like a reasonable request.

Only a few people dropped by, more curious than cordial, and my suite's hors d'oeuvres went practically untouched. It was painfully clear that I was not the popular choice among the power brokers of the party.

The next day's vote would reinforce that as the committee voted to endorse Mark Singel as the opponent for Arlen Specter. Singel received 277 votes. I got six. It was not an encouraging start, but I had no intention of quitting.

There was little doubt that the way to win recognition would be on television, an expensive and effective medium. That meant raising money, lots of it. We set a goal for the primary in excess of $1 million. We would end up with $920,000, enough to buy substantial television time in the six media markets statewide.

I was never comfortable with the conventional solicitation system of politics, sitting at a desk making phone calls to prospects. My style is in-person, one-on-one, or in small groups. I did some of both.

I also loaned some of my own money to the campaign, which led to my personal finances becoming an issue. I was fortunate to have some money of my own, much of which came from my grandfather in Tennessee who had been a successful car dealer and an even wiser investor.

Under pressure to do so, I reluctantly released my tax returns and was embarrassed by the headline, "Yeakel a Millionaire." It should have been something I was proud to announce. Why do we feel we must apologize for any good fortune that comes our way?

The publicizing of my financial circumstances was more than just annoying to me. It was trespassing on my privacy. I wasn't used to that. The tone of the primary campaign, rather mild because we were fellow Democrats, began to grow tense. Mark Singel called me a "limousine liberal" who was only in the race as a hobby, and he persisted in questioning my sincerity and motivation, the cornerstones of my campaign. One Republican television commentator described me as a "Junior Leaguer run amok."

My campaign team had made up our minds early that the focus would be Specter, not Singel. Our quarrel was with what had happened to Anita Hill and with the underrepresentation of women in the Senate. If we were going to appeal to Pennsylvania Democrats, it would have to be on the basis of Lynn Yeakel having a better chance to defeat Specter in November than Singel would have.

My positions on issues were an extension of the work I had done throughout my career. I wanted better health services for women and their families, support systems for older women, counseling and protection for victims of rape and domestic violence, lesbian and gay civil rights, employment fairness for all.

Beyond the issues that had been an everyday pursuit of equitable treatment for women, I had pretty definite views on several hot-button topics. I favored handgun control, and said so. I campaigned for universal health care. I thought the defense budget was too high and the dollars for childhood programs were too low. I opposed the death penalty.

The fence-sitting ability some politicians have, that tight-wire-walking skill that enables them to be on all sides of a given issue, never appealed to me. I was tired of the phrase, "This is the way politics is."

I found campaigning to be exciting one moment, disappointing the next and exhausting almost always. The seven-days-a-week schedule hijacked precious weekend time with family and friends. When I finally got to my hotel/motel room at night, after the last event of the day, I often felt very much alone and was anxious about the unpredictability of the future.

Visiting the towns and villages of rural Pennsylvania was a revelation. I was accustomed to Philadelphia and its suburbs and found huge differences in lifestyles and values in other parts of the state. The crowds, mostly women, grew larger. The TV spots were paying off. More people recognized me. I was moving up in the polls. The press began to ask tougher questions.

Every moment I could find away from rallies and town meetings and making those dreaded fundraising calls, I studied and shaped position papers and worked on my public speaking style. I had been warned early that I needed more "authority" in my voice.

That is another of those criticisms that have dogged women.

Though most of history's great orators have been men, one of the most electrifying speakers of the twentieth century was Barbara Jordan, congresswoman from Texas. At the 1976 Democratic National Convention, nearly three decades before Barack Obama delivered his turning-point talk at a similar Democratic gathering, Barbara Jordan became the first African American to deliver the convention keynote address.

Gifted with a rich, deep voice and schooled brilliantly in the English language, she commanded attention and inspired her audiences. One of her lines—one of many that boosted my resolve—helped me define the kind of campaign I wanted to run in 1992.

She said, in a 1977 speech, *"What the people want is very simple. They want an America as good as its promise."*

That accurately summed up what my life had been about in relation to the rights of women—to be respected, to be allowed to compete in America's places of power, and to be treated with fundamental fairness as equals in all parts of life.

Near the end of the primary campaign I could feel the tide of recognition surging. All those TV ads, all those public appearances, all those handshakes outside factories on cold mornings—they were starting to show a return on investment.

Sometimes the new celebrity bothered me. I could feel the sands of my privacy shifting beneath my feet. But mostly, it was satisfying. It flirted with my ego.

One such moment occurred three days before the primary election. It had been a long day of campaigning. I wedged into a middle seat in the back of a flight from Pittsburgh to Philadelphia. Suddenly, a gallant knight disguised as a flight attendant came into my life.

He was a young man who spoke quietly, "Are you Lynn Yeakel?"

I owned up.

He said, "Come on up front."

It made my day.

The night before the election I had an indication of the outcome when James Carville, at a Clinton rally in Philadelphia, congratulated me and said that their "internals" showed I would win. I wasn't politically sophisticated enough to know exactly what "internals" were, but I knew it was positive.

On election night at the Hilton Hotel in downtown Philadelphia, the same place where nearly three months earlier I had been outvoted 277-6 by the State Committee, my family and I and my merry band of warriors awaited the results of something we had worked so hard to achieve.

The call we were waiting for came in—the concession from a gracious Mark Singel. Then, other calls came, from Pennsylvania Governor Casey, Geraldine Ferraro, New York City comptroller Elizabeth Holtzman, and many others. We had won.

The ballroom scene was thrilling. The smiles, cheers, joy. My opening line was, "We did it!" Not a phrase for the ages, but right for the occasion. After a late night of celebration, there was a 5:00 a.m. knock on my door, a reminder to get to the hairdresser. I was to be interviewed by Katie Couric on NBC's Today Show.

I had butterflies, but they were flying in formation. It was the beginning of what I came to call my out-of-body experience.

CHAPTER 17

Why Is Politics So Personal?

On the day of the Pennsylvania primary election in 1992, I was relaxing at home while voters were deciding if I would be the Democrat to campaign against Senator Arlen Specter for the next six months. I had some calls to return. One was from Arlen. He had called to congratulate me on running a good campaign. It was an odd, but cordial conversation. We were both awaiting the results of our party's primaries. I said something not very creative, like, "Well, I guess this time tomorrow we'll know what lies ahead." His response was equally bland, "Yes, I guess we will." The irony was that he knew a lot more about what was ahead than I did. And he did not wish me luck.

A political campaign is like a long airplane flight—extended periods of soaring to new heights, occasionally interrupted by sudden and sobering turbulence.

I was soaring after my primary victory. The national media awarded me costar billing with Carol Moseley Braun, who had unexpectedly won her primary in Illinois a few weeks earlier, in what they were now calling the Year of the Woman in Politics. For a brief shining moment, one newspaper called me every woman's Rocky.

It wasn't just Carol and me. The campaigns of women in other parts of the country were also getting a boost from the newly generated energy of women, many of whom called for a change in the 98 percent white male U.S. Senate, and a ballot payback for the verbal abuse of Anita Hill during her testimony against Supreme Court nominee Clarence Thomas. As the year went on, other primaries were won by Dianne Feinstein and Barbara Boxer in California and Patty Murray in Washington.

The *New York Times* called Anita Hill the "silent third candidate" in my race against Arlen Specter.

The media generally delighted in pointing out the similarities Senator Specter and I shared.

He wasn't born in Pennsylvania. Neither was I. Kansas for him. Virginia for me. In college, he was elected to Phi Beta Kappa. So was I.

He had a very successful spouse. So did I.

He had two grown children. I had two grown children.

He was prochoice. I was prochoice.

The press also commented on our differences.

They described me as "open, forward, eager, quick to laugh." Of Specter it was written that he was "half shelled, guarded, cautious."

He was a political infighter, they said. I was a political novice.

He was a two-term U.S. Senator. I was an advocate and fundraiser for women's causes.

They could have pointed out one other glaring difference that would have a dramatic effect on how the upcoming campaign was conducted. The difference: I was a woman.

Because of that biological fact, a lot of things happened that I did not expect. Some of them were positive, most of them upsetting, all of them in some fashion related to my trying to change the absurd gender imbalance in the Senate.

I did not expect the campaign to be so brutal in terms of attacks that had nothing to do with the issues in the campaign. I went into the race to be a voice for women and families, to speak out for disadvantaged people, to address problems in education and health care, to do what I could to promote a safe, secure, and prosperous America.

I ended up, however, investing an enormous amount of time and energy defending my church, my husband's choice of golf clubs, my father's congressional record, even the area where I had chosen to live.

The attacks seldom came from Specter himself. He had plenty of surrogates who were uninterested in the truth. The idea was to keep me busy responding to false charges and to get me off-message. It probably worked. I found the personal attacks ugly and, frankly, beside the point, in a contest to decide who could best represent 12 million Pennsylvanians in Washington. I made the mistake of thinking the accusations would not be taken seriously.

Almost worse than the tactic of lies repeated over and over was the acceptance—even among some of my advisors—that this "whatever-it-takes-to-win" attitude was the way to run a campaign.

I believe that as the future number of women candidates increases we will see a lessening of such unchecked recklessness. Politicians in the heat of a campaign, like kids fighting on a playground, are very much in need of supervision by grown-ups.

I also did not expect the surplus of deal-making that was proposed by people who wanted something for something—"I'll bring in this bloc of voters in exchange for your on-the-record support for my agenda." Endorsements were for sale. Once powerful Pennsylvania State Senator Vince Fumo, who's now serving time in jail for abusing privileges of his office, asked if I would promise to appoint "his" judges. I said that I could not make that commitment and Fumo cost me many Philadelphia votes, telling U.S. Senator Harris Wofford, "She won't listen."

When I turned down such deals because in my view they were wrong, I lost votes, lots of them, but I also knew that what I was doing was right.

I could hear the question my political consultant had asked me when we first met, "Do you suffer fools gladly?" I understood that question better as the campaign wore on. I could also hear a voice from the past saying "Women will never make it in politics."

In fact, after I narrowly lost the general election, radio talk show host Mary Mason, who was not an ally during the campaign, said, "You'll never be a politician because you can't fake it." What a sad thought.

Another campaign surprise was that I'd have to raise so much money. For most of 1992 I was either raising money or thinking about it. This was not my father's simple low-cost door-to-door, neighborhood-to-neighborhood campaign. I was up against an entrenched incumbent with a seemingly bottomless canyon full of money and the ability to trade federal grants and earmarks for votes. With twelve years of Senate-related contacts already stockpiled, Specter had a well-oiled funding machine.

Our campaign money came in from people all over Pennsylvania and, as national publicity picked up, from across the country. The checks, though often small, were numerous—fifty-two thousand in all—and eventually added up to most of the five million dollars my campaign spent. Specter would spend $10 million. That $15 million spent over nine months was more than Women's Way had raised in the sixteen years I'd been involved for services to hundreds of thousands of Pennsylvania women and families. Another sad fact about public priorities.

There's a reason that being elected to Congress is about as close as you can come to having guaranteed job security. Every two years in the House, every six years in the Senate, you can hear the same refrain. Polls show public approval of Congress is at an all-time low. Surely, this will be the year we throw the rascals out. Spirited campaigns follow. Debates are staged and dodged. Excitement builds as election day approaches. But when the dust settles and the voting machines are put back in storage, 90-plus percent of incumbents are returned to office.

It's not a fair fight. I have supported candidates for office in Washington with a check. They have won, and before the ink is dry on the headlines proclaiming their victory, long before they raise their arm to take the oath of office, they are calling or writing with their request for campaign funds for an election two years away.

Add a year-round fundraising machine to "pork distribution" finesse, and opponents seeking to unseat an incumbent have odds against them that Las Vegas would take off the board.

"Pork distribution" is another way of describing the delivery of checks from government to community organizations. They are allocated with uncanny timing that happens to coincide with an incumbent's reelection time. There were a number of examples of that in my race, where my natural allies—breast cancer advocates and nurses as two examples—told me that they could not publicly support me because of Senator Specter's influence over their federal grants.

Arlen Specter was a pork producer of awesome dimensions.

I honestly did not expect the media to devote so much coverage to the superficial aspects of the campaign, to the personalities instead of platforms.

Every gesture was criticized. Every word was analyzed. What did she really mean by that? Why did she use that phrase? Does she have a hidden agenda?

There was my voice, which I'd always thought was fine, but one reporter (a woman) described as "high-pitched and lacking authority." If I deliberately corrected it, then sure to follow would be: "What's happened to Lynn Yeakel's voice?"

Some of the words used to describe me were overtly sexist. As an example, one commentator used sports analogies to describe Specter's campaign while using cooking comparisons to describe mine!

My hair, jewelry, and wardrobe were scrutinized daily. Not once did I read or hear an analysis of Arlen Specter's coiffure or his nondescript gray suits, while my staff had to field questions of whether that was a "Dorothy Hamill wedge" cut I was sporting.

Were my skirts too short? Were the colors too bright? Did my clothes appear too expensive and make me look like an elitist? Were they too off-the-rack? A Philadelphia Inquirer Magazine cover story about me was entitled "The Talbots Radical." I had never shopped at Talbots.

I know members of the media are trying to find angles so they can get an edge with readers, listeners, and viewers; but while they were paying attention to my appearance, the issues of poverty, domestic violence, child care, education, health insurance, and other critical matters at stake were being shortchanged.

Advantage: the male candidate.

Another by-product of the campaign I hadn't expected was that I had very little control of my own time.

I certainly had a preview of this circus in the primary, but nothing quite prepared me for the collective demands of a campaign scheduler who insisted on stopping off at one more county fair, of a media manager who had found a middle-of-the-night radio talk show that wanted a guest, of a finance manager who had just one more list of people to call—with about twenty names on it—for contributions, and of a campaign manager letting me know politely but firmly that we were running two hours late. I came to think of myself as a commodity and later realized I had lost my own grounding.

Time with my family was rare, but precious, during this six-month campaign. Time with friends had to be postponed. I kept reminding myself of what so many women had told me: "Somebody has to run against that man."

The most pleasant surprise was how my candidacy mobilized women of all ages, particularly the young. They filled my rallies. They told me that they "finally had someone they could vote for." Many registered and voted for the first time. The look of the future I saw in their eyes encouraged me, told me that what I was going through might have a down-the-road dividend.

One woman told me she came to a rally after telling her husband, a staunch Republican, that she was going somewhere else. It was really part of what we were fighting for—the opportunity for women to take an active role in the political process. If you are for a candidate and feel strongly about him or her, you should have no reluctance to say so and to cast your vote accordingly.

Not all women stood with me. I never expected them to. Some opposed my stand on abortion rights, but my opponent had the same position. In some cases, women could accept that view from a man, but not from another woman. Still other women simply preferred a Republican. I had no quarrel with that. I never considered myself "the woman's candidate," no matter how much the opposing camp tried to marginalize me with that brand.

Perhaps my biggest surprise came in November, when over 2,200,000 Pennsylvania voters who hadn't even heard my name a year earlier stepped into the voters' booths and made me their choice for U.S. Senator. That has always been a gratifying memory. Almost twenty years later strangers stop me in airports or stores or on the street and say, "I worked for you in 1992." And work they did.

Thousands of Pennsylvania women, and many men, stuffed envelopes, served on telephone banks, set up chairs in meeting halls, knocked on the doors of their neighbors, staked out lawn signs; and when the opposition uprooted those signs, they went back and replaced them with fresh ones.

The race had its share of glamour too. My speech to a jam-packed Madison Square Garden at the Democratic National Convention with international TV coverage was certainly a boost for my ego. Reviewing our daily clipping service was a lift. Sharing the same platform with a man who was running for another office that year—Bill Clinton—was an honor.

But throughout the summer and on into the autumn I never forgot my true motivation for running—to bring justice for women a giant step closer.

Left: In the late-'40s, Virginia's new Congressman, Porter Hardy, Jr., gathering his family around him – my mother Lynn, brother Porter III, and that's me at age five.

Right: My dad huddling with President John Kennedy and VP Lyndon Johnson in the early '60s. Dad and JFK entered Congress together in 1947.

Above: In 1960 at Randolph-Macon Woman's College I was organizing Young Democrats for JFK – the man who later, briefly became my dance partner.

Right: My dad, on January 2, 1965, prepared to "give me away" on the day I married Paul and became Lynn Hardy Yeakel.

Left: Working on community issues, as Junior League President (I'm on the right), at the organization's headquarters.

Right: Standing between two heroes for women's rights. The late Ernesta Drinker Ballard (left), was my Women's Way mentor. Business leader Rosemarie Greco later joined me in chairing Vision 2020.

Left: Doing their "Rocky" imitation, Women's Way agency directors and community board members rallied on the landmark steps of the Philadelphia Art Museum.

Right: Chatting with the dynamic singer Helen Reddy before she made a surprise appearance at Women's Way's 10th anniversary dinner and brought 2000 people to their feet cheering her rendition of her signature song, "I Am Woman."

Yeakel for Senate

She has a better sense than Specter of what's wrong — and how to fix it

We endorse Lynn Yeakel over Arlen Specter for the United States Senate, because she supports — albeit

We do not deny the fact that Sen. Specter has been, as he claims, a reliable supporter of women's interests. But the fundamen-

Above: Having a creative time with my underdog run for the Senate in 1992, cartoonists were generally sympathetic.

Left: Starting with only one percent name recognition in Pennsylvania, we flooded the state with get-to-know-me literature.

Right: Riding the campaign bus that would take me to so many places I can't remember and will never forget.

Above: Uniting our enthusiasm, candidates for the U.S. Senate assembled for this photo in the "Year of the Woman," 1992. Non-candidates Ellen Malcolm, president of Emily's List, is second from left, and Geraldine Ferraro is far right (in the picture, never politically!).

Above: Taking a pre-victory walk to the polls with Paul on Primary Election Day in 1992.

Left: Celebrating an upset win over the sitting Lieutenant Governor on April 28, 1992, ending a long uphill primary campaign.

Right: Consulting with Gloria Steinem, a woman of stand-up courage and commitment who came to help me as she has done with so many women.

Below: Cheering at a rally with two highly respected Philadelphia councilwomen, Marian Tasco and Augusta Clark.

Below: In Scranton, in 1992, campaigning with the soon-to-be President Bill Clinton. I would later join his Administration as Regional Director of Health and Human Services in the Mid-Atlantic area.

Right: Speaking at the 1992 Rosemont College Commencement with protestors in the street drowned out by a standing ovation from the students.

Left: Meeting with Hillary Clinton, a woman of incredible strength who is unafraid to take on new challenges.

Right: Guess which one is not a doctor or training to be one? Joining me to salute WOMAN ONE scholarship winners Donyell Doram and Carla Zaballos are Drexel University's College of Medicine executives Dr. Barbara Schindler and Dean Richard Homan.

Left: Encouraging women in the community to take charge of their own health and discover their own leadership potential is critical to the work of Drexel's Institute for Women's Health and Leadership.

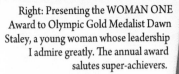

Right: Presenting the WOMAN ONE Award to Olympic Gold Medalist Dawn Staley, a young woman whose leadership I admire greatly. The annual award salutes super-achievers.

Below: "Making a World of Difference" with the staff of the Drexel University College of Medicine Institute for Women's Health and Leadership, where Vision 2020 was born.

Left: Inspiring me to carry out the Vision 2020 work are granddaughters Chloe and Mae who, in the Year 2020 will be 18 and 21, both voting for the first time in a presidential election.

Below: Sitting for a three-generation family portrait that includes husband Paul, daughter Courtney and her husband Martín Arias, son Paul and his wife Pilar, plus my six grandchildren whom I refer to as the 21st Century's first generation.

Right: Visiting Signers' Hall at the National Constitution Center in Philadelphia two centuries later, still wondering, "Where are all the women?"

CHAPTER 18

If We Spend Too Much Time Looking in the Rearview Mirror, Will We Miss Our Turn?

Sometimes I wonder if Dorothy in *The Wizard of Oz* ever looked back thinking she might have done some things differently. She did a lot of things well. She exercised risk-taking by following the Yellow Brick Road despite little available research as to where it would lead. She fought off the negative input of Auntie Em. She outsmarted the enchanted trees, survived a tornado, held the Wizard to his promises. She treated her colleagues well, oiling the Tin Man, encouraging the Lion, rewriting the job description of the Scarecrow. All things considered, she was probably glad she made the trip. I can identify with that.

One of the campaign experiences I truly enjoyed, but which also was the most pressure filled, was my single live television debate with incumbent Senator Arlen Specter.

My campaign wanted more debates. The underdog always does, but Specter's handlers preferred none and agreed to have one. It was important because it gave me an opportunity to be on the same stage with him, to show that I could debate the issues with credibility.

The format was rather mechanical. Moderator asks the question. Candidate No. 1 responds within a time limit. Candidate No. 2 does the same. Next question: same procedure, reverse the order. To me, a direct conversation between the two candidates is a better way to go because it's less rehearsed, and there are fewer practiced sound bites. It is a more open window to what the contestants are really like. Candidates spouting out statistics on tax policies, gross national products, defense budgets, unemployment figures—that is predictable and boring.

As a woman candidate, I particularly wanted an open exchange of ideas and opinions to demonstrate that I had both a command of the facts and the emotional cool to communicate them. These are traits often attributed to a male candidate simply because men have dominated politics since day one.

The debate, which was held in Pittsburgh, went surprisingly well. One media report the next day said, "(Yeakel) more than held her own," and my daughter, Courtney, who was in the studio with the rest of my family, afterward said, "Mom, you kicked ass!" An unexpected opportunity came in the middle of the debate when Specter pulled some papers out of his briefcase under the podium. This was against debate rules, and I turned to the moderator, who called him on it. The next day when I flew back to Philadelphia a group of supporters surprised me at the airport chanting, "2, 4, 6, 8—Lynn has won the great debate!"

But back on a day-to-day basis, belittling my candidacy and implicitly questioning my competency had become key elements in my opponent's game plan. This patronizing pat-on-the-head style was wearing thin on women who felt their access to public leadership should have been secured decades earlier.

For years, women suffragists in pursuit of the most basic of democratic franchises had been subjected to scorn, ridicule, dirty jokes, demeaning cartoons and time in jail. After the hard-won 1920 achievement of the right to vote, the clock was stopped again on the political progress of women. Women didn't push harder for a bigger role in government and the men in power were not about to make room for them at the top.

With one exception. As governor of New York, Franklin D. Roosevelt became impressed by the work of Frances Perkins, a Boston-born social worker who learned about finance and commerce at the University of Pennsylvania's Wharton School and at Columbia.

When Roosevelt became president in the midst of the Depression, he selected Frances Perkins to be Secretary of Labor, the first woman ever to serve in a Cabinet position. Her appointment came only after extended controversy, but she went on to serve with distinction for twelve years.

Even later in the twentieth century, when some measure of progress was being made in other lines of work by women, the road to political power remained under construction, marked by frequent detour signs.

In education, the male/female faculty ratio was improving, and the numbers of women in decision-making administrative posts was growing.

In medicine, women were on the move. As more women graduated from medical school and demonstrated their skills, we seemed to be headed in a direction worth going.

In law, more women were joining established legal firms, arguing cases in court, some becoming partners.

In business, at an almost one-at-a-time pace, women stopped making coffee and started making decisions. There were a scarce few in the boardroom, with a few more in executive management positions. At first they were generally put into "safe" positions, like heading up human resources or public relations. Later, but still rarely, women emerged in finance, even engineering, and—on occasions so infrequent they earned large type on the business page—some women became CEOs.

The barriers to political power for women and the unacceptable 98-2 gender imbalance in the U.S. Senate were all in place when I ran my Senate race in 1992. Public opinion then, which is thankfully changing, was that women simply aren't suited to the rough and tumble that is American politics, that we may not be strong enough as a gender to stand up to world leaders.

Tell that to Eleanor Roosevelt, Madeleine Albright, Condoleezza Rice, or Hillary Clinton. Tell it to Margaret Thatcher. Or to Golda Meir, who will be forever on my list of women heroes for her response to a curfew placed on women because of an outbreak of street violence against them. She asked, "If the violence is being committed by men, shouldn't they be the ones to be subject to a curfew?"

Give me a government where half the seats are filled with women, and I'll show you a government that is more sensitive to the needs of families and communities and almost certainly more inclined to peacemaking.

When I won the primary, the *New York Times* called me a "maverick," the popular political label for someone who is independent, does not necessarily follow party lines or conventional wisdom. I accepted it as a compliment, in part because it recalled my father's reputation, but I have never really thought that campaigning for women to have equal footing with men in the arena of citizenship is particularly rebellious.

The American public needs to understand, as many people do now, that women have come too far to turn back. We are not going away from the political table. We've taken too many bumps and bruises to get there.

I recall a popular query among my colleagues when 1992 was called the Year of the Woman was "Do you mean we only get one?"

Clearly, Arlen Specter did not want to give us even one.

I had been warned about his political tactics. He had chaired Nixon's 1972 reelection run in Pennsylvania and was from the Richard Nixon school of campaigning. Specter would later say that I was the toughest candidate he ever faced, although he may want to revisit that position since he switched parties and was defeated by Joe Sestak in the 2010 Democratic primary. Specter was determined "to do what it took" to win. I was amused when he later authored a book with the title, *Passion for Truth*. That must have been a passion of more recent acquisition because there was little evidence of it in 1992, and truth seemed to be irrelevant to his campaign.

No distortion hurt more than the McCarthy-style "guilt by association" tactic of implying, based on a sermon once preached by the pastor of my church and taken entirely out of context, that since I was a member, I was anti-Semitic. I naively thought that because these charges were completely outrageous and unfounded, no one would believe them.

Wasn't I the person who proposed the first Jewish woman for membership in the Junior League of Philadelphia? Wasn't I a leader in building Women's Way on a foundation of zero prejudices? Not to mention the fact that many of my campaign staff, my campaign manager, close friends, and staunchest supporters were Jewish.

And the verbal assaults continued into the country club where my husband played golf. There were no black members. Therefore the inference was that it must be racist, although there was no discriminatory membership policy. At almost every appearance I made in public, there were Specter people planted in the audience, eager to repeat the lies in the form of attack questions.

This strategy was not only politics at its mean-spirited worst, but it was also divisive and played upon people's fears. It's the kind of political recklessness that discourages many capable people from running for office.

I had hoped that the media would help put a stop to this constant harassment. Reporters like to think of themselves as watchdogs who study politicians and alert the public to any kind of misbehavior. That's how they want to be regarded.

I found out, though, that instead of becoming watchdogs, they often end up being lapdogs, too easy to coax into printing stories before verifying the facts.

In the movie *"Absence of Malice,"* Paul Newman played a character who had been wrongly maligned in a newspaper story by a reporter played by Sally Field. He asked her if she liked what she did for a living. She responded that she wrote the truth, to which he said, "You don't write the truth. You write what people say."

The urge to turn Specter's tactics back on him kept building within my campaign. Every day there seemed to be a new reason to counter his charges with some headline grabbers of our own. Staff members begged me to get nasty. I refused. That's not why I was running for office, and I simply would not believe that such tactics were the only route to political power. I never have understood the tolerance for taking the low road in politics. It confounds me that behavior that is unacceptable in other parts of life is seemingly routine on the campaign circuit.

The quest for a "fair fight"—a contest in which both sides value ethics—is the refrain I hear from many women in politics. They say,—"Let us compete. Let us retire the win-at-any-cost campaign style. If that's naïve, then so be it."

It's difficult to figure out what the media think is worth covering and what they choose to ignore. In my race against Specter there had been rumors, open conversations, even eyewitness accounts of a "river of money" flowing out of the Specter campaign onto the streets of Philadelphia and Pittsburgh. A reporter in Philadelphia had the story, but refused to pursue it.

Veteran political observers called it "old news." Newcomers to politics, most of us women, kept asking, "Is this the way it has to be?"

I am not a fan of second-guessing my own choices. "Don't look backward unless that's where you're planning to go" is still good advice.

However, as I went to the polls to vote on election day, I permitted myself a brief look-back question—after the ten most hectic months of my life, if I were to do it all over, would I do anything differently?

Would I have run? No doubt about it. Anita Hill, 98-2, women shut out of the process, lack of ethical standards of conduct. Somebody had to make a statement.

Would I have set aside my principles to win the prize by any means available? No way. To do that is to forfeit one's own integrity.

One other question that morning—would I be able to deal with the outcome, win or lose?

I'd know in a few hours. Or perhaps in a few years.

CHAPTER 19

How Can We Find Victory and Reject Victimhood?

Every year as the seasons grudgingly change from winter to spring, America experiences a phenomenon called "March Madness." It's the annual college basketball tournament where sixty-five teams compete for the top prize, the national championship. Reality says that sixty-four of those teams will end their seasons with a loss, will feel the sting of defeat. That leaves them one more challenge—finding a way to keep it all in perspective, to understand that they competed well to get this far, that the game was fair, and that perhaps, by example, they inspired others to chase the same goal.

Ellen Goodman is one of my favorite journalists. Her columns were on my must-read list since long before she wrote about me in between my primary election victory and the November vote for the U.S. Senate seat from Pennsylvania.

She has an enviable ability to capture a message, package it, and deliver it to the reader with clarity and simple semantic elegance.

Ellen Goodman said so well what I was trying to bring to the voters:

> *There has been a serving of good cheer in the voting booth . . . Until now we've all been told that people are voting with a sour taste in their mouths . . . Their appetite has been dampened by disappointment and disillusionment . . . They've been fed a steady diet of the same old gruel . . . Lynn Yeakel has provided a nice change of flavor.*

The core of her column was not praise of me, but rather a ringing recognition that the seemingly sudden emergence of women who were politically competitive was the result of groundwork that had been going on for years. Politics had finally become the next phase of women's expanding influence. As the *New York Times* editorialized, over a large photo of my primary victory night celebration on the Sunday of Memorial Day weekend 1992, "Sisterhood is Political."

Of all the major women candidates for the U.S. Senate in the "Year of the Woman," I faced the toughest odds. Some were running for open seats, and Carol Moseley Braun had defeated the incumbent in the Illinois primary. My opponent was entrenched, determined, and had twice the money I did. I was unwilling to make old line political deals, and I was toe-to-toe with the sheer power of a system that was front-loaded for the incumbent.

As my energized supporters gathered at the Hilton Hotel in Philadelphia to await the November election results, we had every right to believe we had conducted a good campaign. We kept to the issues. We resisted the opportunity to take the low road. Either we were going to win on the merits of our positions or we were going to lose with our heads held high.

I have never been an "ends-justify-the-means" person.

Years later, when I made runs for Pennsylvania governor and the state senate, I maintained that refusal to engage in personal attacks. To some, the sleaze factor may be a winning strategy, but I simply don't feel we get anywhere positive as a human race by buying into that.

I asked myself additional questions as the early returns came in and showed a predictable lead over Specter from the heavily Democratic Philadelphia reporting districts.

Did we wake up women to the possibility of achieving political power?

I think so. We had clear indications that women who had never ventured into the political process were writing checks, stuffing envelopes, attending rallies, getting out the word, staying informed on the issues.

Did I speak out on what was important?

As near as I could recall, for over six months at every stop, in every interview, in front of every audience, I talked of equality for all people, about access to a good education and health care, about a more caring government that would include women and listen to voices that had been silent for so long.

Were the tough issues handled without compromise?

Yes, I felt good about that. I believe in gun control and I knew that in Pennsylvania that position would cost me votes. I've always felt it was a matter of good sense. If we license automobiles and take away driving privileges when traffic laws are violated, why shouldn't we license guns and take away those privileges when their use is abused?

I don't know whether serious gun control legislation will ever be enacted in Pennsylvania, but people who feel strongly about it should continue to speak up. I had seen the results of gun violence in Philadelphia, and I was not about to back away from my position on the issue. Though I was never a threat to Pennsylvania sports enthusiasts, the powerful National Rifle Association lobby targeted my candidacy and poured money into Arlen Specter's campaign.

Even as the votes were being counted that night in November, I still thought about my disgust and disappointment at the discovery that there are no standards of conduct for candidates—no rules to govern behavior, no machinery to enforce fairness. Candidates regularly make misleading claims about their own records and inflammatory charges against their opponents.

Part of the problem is that the public becomes so numbed by the deluge of lying, they think a politician is lying even when he or she is telling the truth. I still recall a *New York Times* commentary saying that in the U.S. Congress, lying is a way of life, and everyone knows it, and everyone accepts it. Besides, the attack ads work, driving up an opponent's negatives.

How can it be that we've reached this point as a society? How can we entrust our lives, our national security, our environment, the spending of our tax dollars, our children's futures, to people who routinely deceive us?

The evening moved along slowly as my lead in the vote count began to slow in Philadelphia. This was not good news since I needed to counter the upstate numbers Specter was sure to get. My staff was still working only on victory remarks, refusing to accept that a concession talk might be a possibility.

I continued to field questions in my mind.

Did my position on reproductive choice help me or hurt me?

Probably both. I was for a woman's right to choose. I was asked about it often. My opponent, whose position was identical with mine, was seldom, if ever, asked. I wondered, and still do, why women candidates are questioned more intently on sensitive subjects than men are. And why is a prochoice woman more threatening to some than a man who believes the same thing?

Did I raise money the right way?

I thought so, although I hated doing it. People from throughout America sent checks—and with many came messages of encouragement: "go get 'em" and "thanks for running against the odds." I remember running into actor Robin Williams in New York during the Democratic convention, and he said, "Kick ass, Lynn!" So many supporters told me that if I won, all women won. And if I lost, all women had moved a step forward because I had tried.

That made me reflect on the message we had attempted to communicate. I had urged women to join me in unity of purpose, not uniformity of opinion. Differences are precious, but they can be integrated. Helen Keller said it so simply: "Alone we can do so little. Together we can do so much."

The essential element of progress that we women make does not rely upon our common thoughts, but the results we produce through an open process of trial and error, of debate and growth.

It was getting late, and those troublesome veteran poll watchers were letting me know that the trend was not favorable. We were going to lose by a margin narrow enough that we might second-guess ourselves for years to come if we allowed it.

Rewriting our own history so that the fantasy is more enjoyable than the fact is something women have been doing for years, even centuries. I was not going to participate in that game. Part of what we had been trying to do all these months was to empower women to be in charge of their own lives so that dreaming up a different outcome in their work, their relationships, their goal seeking, would not be necessary.

As painful as it was to lose the election, as exhausted as I was after all those bumpy flights, hurry-up meals and fundraising calls, and as sad as I was to go downstairs in the hotel to talk to the media and my loyal supporters, I was not into regrets.

There was little time for feeling sorry for myself anyway. Election protocol required the sequential rituals of making the dreaded phone call to my opponent, putting on my bravest face to go before the TV cameras, and thanking my tearful friends, many still in denial.

Neither my call to Specter nor my message to those gallant warriors carried words for the ages. To him, I remember saying I was glad it was over. To them, I probably said that sometimes there is a victory in defeat. I know

I included in those remarks a reference to the "somebody said it couldn't be done" homily, saying, "We tried!"

My comments were sincere, especially my heartfelt appreciation to my supporters around the state, but there was no joy in putting up the good fight only to lose a close race. I do not like to lose—not at chess, not at bridge, and certainly not in an election I considered to be so keenly important to the issues that had been dominating my life for twenty years.

When I returned to my hotel room, it felt more like an island than a room. After being surrounded by bustling crowds of well-wishers for nearly a full year, I was alone. My family had gone home, my campaign staff was drowning their sorrows in a room down the hall. The moments of peace I had sought during the campaign suddenly seemed like hours of isolation. All that serenity I thought would be so welcome became more turbulent than tranquil.

There would be no *Today* show appearance the next morning, no national press calling for interviews, no requests from political powerbrokers asking about open jobs for their relatives on my Washington staff.

I thought again how forcefully the establishment had united behind Specter to hold his Senate seat. It was done by a combination of Republican strength and some people in high places in my own party crossing over to preserve the status quo. There were old alliances, deals and promises that existed behind the scenes.

What was that dilemma I had recited so often? Oh yes, what makes "change" so difficult in Washington is that the power of change lies in the hands of people who have the greatest stake in keeping things the way they are.

The morning after the election two of my friends were there to keep me from wallowing in self-pity. I kept it together as we walked over to campaign headquarters until a young woman who was clearly on her way to work recognized me, stopped and said, "Your loss is our loss." At that point I burst into tears. When we reached the office, it was already being cleaned out. Still remaining were never-to-be-used lawn signs and bumper stickers, a year full of memories, and a staggering campaign debt that would take me four years to resolve.

The night after the election, another of my there-when-you-need-her friends took me to the annual Philadelphia Craft Show Preview, a big event that we had attended together for several years. I remember wandering through the booths in a daze, accepting condolences. I found myself wanting to go home and begin picking up the pieces with my family.

At home, there were flowers from thoughtful people. And messages that thankfully were not consolation, but congratulations for having tried to climb the mountain, for setting an example for young girls, and for bringing so many women out of the wilderness of passivity into the arena of action.

Then the phone rang. The call was from a person I had never met, but she had been my sister for the past ten months. It was Anita Hill, calling to thank me for "speaking up to power." She had not called during the campaign, she said, because it didn't seem appropriate to do so. It was certainly appropriate—and welcomed—now.

If I had ever wondered for a minute why I risked so much to run this race, her call cleared away the wonder. If I had ever doubted for a second the worth of what I was doing, her call eliminated the doubt. She was gracious and appreciative of my high-risk campaign which she told me she had closely followed.

I knew there was misery yet to be endured in the days ahead, but in addition to the ache, there was satisfaction in remembering many special moments I had experienced that made our campaign slogan, "Courage for a Change," so meaningful.

One of those memorable moments happened just a few blocks away from my home, in the middle of the campaign, at a commencement ceremony that could never be classified as "just another college graduation."

CHAPTER 20

How Do We Define Courage?

Some people believe that women can't change politics, that politics will change women. I disagree. I believe we can improve the electoral process, as well as the way we legislate and govern. What it takes is enough women with the courage and will to work hard, to make citizenship a priority. We need to stand together in the heat *outside* the kitchen.

I never knew Ida May Fuller. I wish I had. She probably would have bolstered frequent arguments I've had with my conservative friends about the value of a compassionate government in people's lives.

Ida May Fuller was the first American to receive a Social Security check. She was a retiree living in Vermont. The year was 1940 and Social Security had been introduced into the American way of life only after a long and vigorous scrimmage in Washington. Ida May's first check was for $22.54.

She would live another thirty-five years and amass total lifetime Social Security payments of $22,000. Not much by today's numbers, but that check, regardless of its size, helped her live out her life with dignity. It was there for her every month. Something she could count on.

The debate over how much or how little government we should have usually comes around to the question of how "big" is big? As popular as it is on the political platform to make "big government" the bad guy of choice during a campaign, when you examine America's obligations, "big" isn't all that bad.

To criticize an institution just because it's large is to overlook the fact that without "big," a lot of important things just don't get done.

It took a big military to win World War II.

It took big business to build the industrial strength of a nation and put over 100 million people to work.

It took big systems to manage a program like Medicare that helps preserve the health of a country's population.

Big agriculture produces food supplies we take for granted and big education keeps us technologically and intellectually competitive in the world.

Even big oil, which is a popular target for criticisms from any politician worth his weight in finger pointing, can claim a good deal of credit for fueling, heating and lighting America.

So "big" has its place, although I don't ascribe to the notion that a business can be "too big to fail." When "bigness" becomes arrogant or abusive, that's when we find out who has the courage to say so.

In the matter of restricting women's rights, I have found the foe is often more difficult to identify, sometimes as sinister as it is elusive. An almost "silent system" developed in the first couple of American centuries with many collaborators quietly cooperating to "keep women in their place," and whatever "place" that was, women would not have a vote to choose it.

That's why I always have admired specific acts of courage taken by women despite the presence of considerable risk. One such woman was Ofelia Garcia, who in the spring of 1992, stood as tall as the job description for hero could possibly require.

Keep in mind that in May of that year I was leading a high profile life as a first-time political candidate who had just won the Democratic nomination for U.S. Senator.

I had been invited earlier that year to be the commencement speaker at Rosemont College, a Catholic college for women located in the Main Line area just outside Philadelphia.

Rosemont was a highly respected educational institution. I was an admirer of what it had achieved, and I was then, and still am, supportive of all-women colleges. I was thrilled to be invited to speak at the graduation ceremonies, but also surprised, because in my previous leadership role at Women's Way, I had become somewhat of a lightning rod with the Archdiocese of Philadelphia because of my advocacy for women's reproductive rights.

Ofelia Garcia was inaugurated as Rosemont's tenth president just a month before the 1992 commencement.

Her career in art and academics included Havana, New York, Boston, Atlanta, and Philadelphia. She was a political exile from Cuba and an educator who made it clear that her expectations were for Rosemont students to do more than their share to improve the world around them.

"In all measurable ways," she said, "women from women's colleges achieve better results than those from coeducational institutions. A Rosemont woman should understand that if ever she accomplishes all she had planned for herself then she has not planned enough."

Predictably, protests over my selection as speaker began almost immediately and they included a letter from the Cardinal to the college. I realized the pressure that Ofelia must have been under to withdraw the invitation. I expected the "we're sorry" call at any minute. It never came.

The talk I had prepared had nothing to do with the prochoice position I held. This was a day to honor the graduates, to encourage them to find a commitment to serve others, to discover the value of self-reliance. My talk would be about them. This was their day, not mine.

Before the ceremony, outside the campus, there were pickets and police. The protest chants were loud. There was a standing-room-only crowd in the hall, including the national press, and I asked Ofelia, "Do you usually have this many people?" She said, "I don't know. This is my first commencement here."

I reminded myself that she had been through a revolution. A few picket signs were not likely to rattle her.

The graduation came off without incident. The speech went well, particularly the part where I said:

"Women need not apologize for our successes. We don't have to apologize for our high standards, our creativity, our multiple interests. We don't have to apologize for being 52 percent of the population. Instead we must stand up for our values and our beliefs."

The stand-up woman of the day was still to be heard from, and shortly thereafter in a letter to all "friends of Rosemont," published in the alumnae magazine, Ofelia Garcia would spell out her reasons for taking a stand in the storm.

Parts of that letter should be on everyone's required reading shelf:

> The choice of Lynn Yeakel as commencement speaker this year thrust
> Rosemont into the headlines and nightly news reports . . . Let me say to
> all that she was selected to speak at our graduation because she is herself
> a graduate of a women's college and . . . has a distinguished record in
> public service, particularly in a variety of programs for women.
>
> Most of the concern comes from those who believe that her
> prochoice views should disqualify her from speaking at Rosemont.
> Let me assure you that Rosemont is proud of its Catholic tradition

and intent on maintaining it, but we do not see difference of ideas or opinions as threatening. We are confident that our community understands that she was invited not because she is prochoice, but in spite of it. No Catholic today can possibly be ignorant of our church's position on abortion, and it is not our intent to provide a forum on campus for this divisive issue. Neither church nor society has been able to resolve it. Rosemont can hardly hope to do so.

Lynn Yeakel is not a "single issue" person and we are not "single issue" Catholics. She, as other speakers before her, was invited to campus for what we admire in her, because of her long record of support for programs such as those for battered women and because today she speaks persuasively for the inclusion of women in government.

External pressure is inappropriate and goes to the core of our standing as a college . . . we can only serve our students and the church if we don't become less of a college for being Catholic.

Most important, all of us wished to make sure that this event would be a celebration for the Class of 1992. The graduates, in their standing ovation for Lynn Yeakel, assured us that they had heard correctly.

As personally gratifying as the standing ovation was, along with the roses that many graduating seniors dropped in my lap as they crossed the stage to receive their diplomas, the real message for me was the confirmation that women were "getting there" in terms of respect for each other. I felt confident that these students were growing up with a sense of their own independence and a determination to recognize the same trait in others. Generation by generation, we make progress.

The story of Ofelia Garcia doesn't end there. Three years later, she resigned from the top job at Rosemont in the wake of another controversy. Four members of the board objected to a campus art exhibit Ofelia planned to bring to Rosemont to illustrate society's treatment of women.

To her, art was a dramatic form of communication. She had previously been president of Atlanta College of Art. She trusted art, but this exhibit, called "Foundations: Underwear/Under Where?" featured an assortment of bras, corsets, and bikinis fashioned from controversial materials—"not suitable for Rosemont" said the protestors.

Though the board did not overturn Ofelia's decision out of respect for her control over academic issues, she felt she could not adequately carry out her duties as president without its full support.

In resigning, she pointed out that only four trustees were upset by the exhibit, but they were the same people who had consistently disagreed with her decisions throughout her tenure. Her action in standing by me as her commencement speaker was cited again as an issue that created tension with some board members. Ironically, Rosemont College benefitted unexpectedly from the controversy. The national publicity surrounding my appearance actually resulted in an increase in out-of-state applicants for admission. In subsequent years, I ran into several women who told me they had chosen Rosemont for just that reason!

There is probably not a whole lot of merit in trying to define courage. Those who have it know what it is. Those who don't can never truly know it. To me, Ofelia Garcia embodied courage.

In an unusual postscript to my Rosemont Commencement experience, the next year—months after I had lost the election and attempted to return to my private life—I was invited to speak at Boston University Law School's graduation, where my daughter and son-in-law were to graduate. I accepted, and two weeks before the ceremony, to my amazement and my family's horror, one of Arlen Specter's right wing supporters who had harassed me during the Senate campaign threatened to organize a protest among Jewish students at the law school. Though the demonstration never materialized, these events confirmed for me that the campaign mud would continue to follow me and I would probably never have true personal privacy again.

"Connecting" has consistently been the centerpiece of getting significant things done in my life.

I like connecting people and issues—issues that matter and people who are not afraid to do something positive about them.

I like connecting problems that need solutions with people who have the will and the resources to solve them.

I like connecting worthy underfunded causes with worthy well-funded people who believe in care and compassion.

And I like to make the connection between courage and change.

"Change" should not be a scary circumstance for women. For most women, change is probably for the better given how women were once treated and how we are now making more of our own decisions.

The reason courage and change are a matched set is that you really can't have change without the courage to bring it about. Likewise you can't demonstrate your stand-up courage without introducing change into your behavior. It is my belief that you can run from problems for years, but sooner or later you will have to take a stand to do what you can to change things that need changing.

My pattern has been to try to do that sooner *and* later.

The 1992 political campaign established wall-to-wall connections for me as I connected with . . .

. . . thousands of people I otherwise would not have met. Years later I remain surprised and pleased by strangers who recognize me from the campaign.

. . . many women who were in need of just the right nudge to spark their involvement in the political process.

. . . fundraising experience which bolstered my confidence that I could steer major funds toward causes that deserved them.

. . . issues women care about, renewing my conviction that when we work together, immovable objects cannot stand against our irresistible force.

. . . important and influential people like the Clintons—Bill and Hillary. I shared some campaign platforms with him and spent time with her on a bus traveling across Pennsylvania, at breakfast diners and chicken dinners.

I did not return to Women's Way. I had some political adventure to get out of my system. I traveled, gave speeches, and spent time with young women especially on college campuses. I coanchored an all-women radio talk show. Whatever I did, the focus was the same—women and justice. I stayed with the game plan.

I met with Donna Shalala, the first cabinet appointee in the new Clinton administration. She talked to me about a job. Everything about what she said seemed to suggest a new path for helping women and families. I listened.

CHAPTER 21

Controversy—Where Would We Be Without It?

A strong leader, male variety, is often applauded for his decisive nature, his assertiveness, his willingness to mix it up on controversial issues. A woman with the same qualities has historically stirred emotional upset for involving herself in "unladylike" behavior. Some people shy away from controversy because they don't understand the word. "Controversy" merely means "a discussion in which opposing opinions clash." There's nothing wrong with that, for man or woman. We don't always argue because we're mad—we argue because we have different goals.

Women's behavior has been governed and judged by long-entrenched rules of conduct. Professionally, when I first entered the workforce in the mid-1960s, women were expected to have lunch with other women. That's just the way it was. To do otherwise was seen as trying to flirt your way up the corporate ladder.

I grew up with heavy emphasis on women's proper roles in society. The guidelines were quite specific:

- Be polite, helpful, and considerate of others.
- Let the man in your life, be it father or husband, take the lead.
- Serve family, neighborhood, church, and community, always putting yourself last.
- Speak at appropriate moments on suitable topics, and avoid arguments or contrary points of view, especially at the dinner table.
- Allow men to pay the checks, open doors, and get off the elevator last.

- Be attractive physically but avoid making the first move.
- Be charming and chatty in social settings, taking care to stay away from issue-oriented discussions.

Until Title IX came along to open up organized athletics for girls, "find a husband" was the major sanctioned sport available to women. It was assumed during my growing-up time that females were born with a genetic inclination to please. We learned that men would make the decisions that guide our lives. Our assignment was to provide the support system for them.

High on that assignment list was the avoidance of any kind of controversy. Though it was okay for men, it was off limits for women. Just look at my Rosemont College commencement speech as late as 1992. Letters, phone calls, protestors, picket signs, media overload—that's what greeted my appearance, because of my position on a woman's right to choose.

Men with the identical stance on the issue—Mayor Ed Rendell of Philadelphia, my friend Senator Harris Wofford, even my political foe Arlen Specter—had all made speeches at Rosemont without incident. The "rules" for women were different. As one of the Rosemont nuns said to me, "It's not your position. It's your gender."

Somehow a man with a prochoice position was less threatening than a woman who stood up for abortion rights. It seems that every breakthrough, large and small, by women in the pursuit of equal treatment, has been accompanied by ridicule, name-calling, and humiliation.

Many men in power seem to assume, by virtue of their "maleness," that they're entitled to hoard that power. They talk mainly to people who think as they do, while women are more inclined, in my experience, to seek a wide mix of views. We like to weigh different opinions and assemble diverse coalitions. We may simply be less afraid of public conflict than men because we are more open to new ideas. Research shows than "undecided" voters are more likely to be women than men.

Couples in which both parties are independent have historically been rare. American history, recent edition, is probably unimaginable without the Clintons.

People who dabble in the parlor game of "what if" find it easy to ask, "What if Bill Clinton had not won the Presidency in 1992 and introduced America to eight years of high drama?" My answer is that he would have been right back there in 1996, and much of the turbulence of that time would merely have been delayed four years.

Men and women who virtually thrive on controversy are seldom far from it.

The high intensity political names of the twentieth century—people who had the winning combination of ego, determination and the ability to communicate in commanding style—were Roosevelt, Kennedy, Reagan, and Clinton.

Love them or not, and they all had their detractors, they had undeniable appeal, unquestioned verbal skills, and a heaping portion of that elusive quality we like to call charisma. Some others who reached the White House may have been in need of some of these attributes. These four seem to have been born with the stuff.

Perhaps the biggest difference of the Clinton era was the partner he brought to Washington. Hillary Rodham Clinton was a professional attorney, a thoroughly independent individual with ideas, a sphere of influence, and a power concept all her own.

Eleanor Roosevelt was a pioneer of civil rights.

Jacqueline Kennedy was a woman of international elegance.

Nancy Reagan was a traditional first lady.

Each had her own strengths.

Hillary Clinton came to Washington with an agenda. She had long demonstrated her commitment to improving the lives of women and children and she had ambitions for acquiring the authority to change things for the better. In terms of the emergence of women leaders on the national scene, she had the wind at her back and for two decades has kept it there.

Not every woman automatically aligns with Hillary Clinton. That was evident in the 2008 Democratic primary battle with Barack Obama, but though some may disagree with her policies or her manner, few can deny that she is a woman who is in tune with what she believes an independent woman ought to be.

The price for her belief, not surprisingly, is controversy.

Controversy over her early attempts to introduce a national health care reform plan to a country that wasn't ready for it quite yet . . . over her action or inaction during the scandal surrounding her husband's behavior with a White House intern . . . over her decision to run for the U.S. Senate in New York, where she had not been a resident . . . over the campaign she ran for the Democratic nomination for President, a run that would attract 18 million primary voters.

And there was controversy over her subsequent endorsement of Obama, which she made despite the protests of many women who had supported her. Her ability to bite her lip after a bitter defeat and eventually to convince millions of her followers to vote for Obama made possible his history-making victory in November of 2008. That's called leadership—doing what you feel is right regardless of the heat you take.

Bill Clinton loved being president, though some of his predecessors found the job confining. Harry Truman expressed his feelings about the annoying part of being president: "There's always somebody coming to dinner."

Clinton enjoyed the world stage. Hillary did also, and still does. The picture of two such strong leaders in the same household was unprecedented in the White House. No other first family generated so much ink—favorable and unfavorable.

Leadership has a lot of luggage. When you make the decision to lead, or try to lead, anything—a Girl Scout troop, your local School Board, a protest against an example of unfairness, a political entity—what goes with that decision is a guaranteed measure of criticism.

Strong leaders do not shrink from controversy. The minute they do, they no longer deserve the "leadership" label they've been given.

I will always be indebted to Mary Watson.

In the rural and conservative center of the Commonwealth of Pennsylvania, in large part because of Mary's efforts, my campaign surprised people by carrying five counties I was not expected to win.

Coming from the Philadelphia suburbs, it was thought there was little chance I could compete in central Pennsylvania. Mary Watson did not accept that. She was a woman of boundless energy and matching optimism. She mobilized an army of volunteers. I remember they wore T-shirts with a quote from one of my early speeches: "Come dream what I dream!"

Most of Mary's recruits were women, many of them were Republicans, and the majority had never been politically active. In fact, some had to hide my promotional literature from their husbands.

In the process of being of enormous value to my campaign, Mary and her amazing warriors learned something about themselves. They discovered that when women unite behind a cause we believe in, we can accomplish some astonishing outcomes.

For so much of our lives we are told that we "have to know when to quit." I believe it's more important to know when *not* to quit.

The disappointment of my political loss was profound. Sadly, it intimidated some of my women supporters into retreating to safe, nonwavemaking lifestyles, believing that this was confirmation that we simply couldn't beat the system. It was hard not to take it personally.

For a while I entertained my own state of shock. There were a number of significant obstacles to overcome. There was the money I had lost, the job I had given up, the unfair mud that had been thrown at my reputation and continued to follow me. I had to remind myself again that this wasn't about me. It was about committing my life to its real purpose—standing up for and empowering other women.

With that in mind, the invitation from the Clinton administration to become Regional Director of Health and Human Services seemed to be a good opportunity for the next phase of my mission.

And that's what it turned out to be.

CHAPTER 22

Can We Learn to Embrace Change That Will Help Us?

We've never done it before. We've been doing it this way for years. We can't take the chance. We're doing okay now as it is. It will never work in this environment. It's too radical a change. I don't want to get involved. We've tried that before. My boss won't like it. It's against policy. Why don't we appoint a committee to study it?

The tool kit for standing still comes with a full set of excuses. To bring about change, you need a counter kit from which you can build your own courage. Some assembly required.

Donna Shalala is a leader with many talents and achievements.

She has taken on challenges that demand a blend of visionary skills and a day-to-day management style that motivates people and accelerates productivity.

She demonstrated her talent as president of the University of Wisconsin at Madison, and later in the top job at the University of Miami. She also proved her leadership as the Secretary of the U.S. Department of Health and Human Services, managing over sixty thousand people and helping meet the needs of millions of Americans who depend upon the wisdom of decisions made and efficiency of operation in this important government agency.

When Bill Clinton became president, naming Donna to HHS was among his first actions.

HHS is the home of Medicare and Medicaid, the Food and Drug Administration, the Centers for Disease Control and Prevention, the National Institutes of Health and its multiple research projects, and a structure built to provide that seven-letter experience called "s-e-r-v-i-c-e."

After the 1992 election, and Donna's appointment, I went to Washington to see her. We had a mutual friend who had already joined her at HHS. I learned that Donna had supported my campaign through Emily's List, and I thought she might have advice for my next career. I was surprised and pleased when she offered me the position of Regional Director for HHS Region III, the Mid-Atlantic states of Pennsylvania, Delaware, Maryland, Virginia and West Virginia, plus the District of Columbia.

The invitation meant a White House appointment and I joined the Department in 1994. By that time, I was ready for a new adventure. This appeared to be an opportunity to pursue goals I had set to improve the lives of women and families—goals that were, happily, aligned with those of the fledgling Clinton administration. At the same time, I was somewhat concerned about taking a "government job." I had been warned about the wilderness of governmental bureaucracy and, realizing that I had an entrepreneurial personality, I did not want to be swallowed up by layers of hierarchy.

To Donna Shalala's credit, she demonstrated the very best characteristics of what is thought of as "women's strengths" in management style. She was firm but fair. She assembled a team that looked like America in terms of gender, age and race. And she empowered her team members, including those of us who headed the Regional Offices.

A landmark piece of legislation, introduced by then-Senator Joe Biden of Delaware, had been signed into law by President Clinton shortly before I assumed my position at HHS. It was the Violence Against Women Act (VAWA), part of the Crime Bill, which for the first time at the federal level recognized violence against women as both a crime and a public health problem. The committee set up to oversee implementation of the new law was cochaired by Donna Shalala and U.S. Attorney General Janet Reno. I joined the national committee in its formative months, the only regional HHS representative to do so. This was an issue I cared passionately about. There were two domestic violence agencies that were members of Women's Way and I had advocated on their behalf for public funds to address the problem.

Among the early outcomes of implementation of the new federal law was the establishment of a national emergency hotline for victims. It was similar to the Philadelphia area hotlines that had served as lifesaving intervention tools for nearly two decades. I was struck by how many strategies developed by early grassroots community advocates had finally made their way to the nation's policymakers, and I was dismayed that it took so long for these solutions to percolate up.

In many ways, the HHS position, and the leadership of President Clinton and Secretary Shalala, gave me a different vantage point. For years I had been hounding both the private and public sectors to step up to the plate for women and families. Now they had handed me a bat and told me that I was the designated hitter for the Mid-Atlantic Region, representing an administration that placed an appropriately high value on our nation's domestic challenges. Serving as Secretary Shalala's liaison to governors and agencies in my assigned territory gave me an opportunity to advocate these views with top decision makers at the state level.

The Mid-Atlantic Regional Office in Philadelphia, with 450 federal employees, administered the many facets of health and human service obligations to the disadvantaged, the aging, and the disabled. To me that was half the mission. The other half of my leadership challenge was to change the work culture so that systems and people would be more productive and happier with their jobs. I had no intention of being a caretaker of the status quo.

A learning curve awaited me.

I had to learn to relate to a geographically and politically diverse group of people and resources—several of the governors I dealt with were Republicans and did not agree with the Clinton administration's priorities.

I also had to learn to work with people who knew more than I did about the system—most of whom had been around a long time, and some who were prepared to educate me on "doing things the way they've always been done around here," just in case I had some ideas about making changes—which I did.

And I had to learn to supervise men. I had never managed men before, except for the illusion of doing so during my political ventures. I found that in a campaign so many decisions were made on the run, it was hard to be certain of who was giving orders and who was following them.

I would come to the conclusion during my five years with HHS that men are often easier to work with than women. They seem to require less emotional investment, possibly because they have fewer competing responsibilities at home. If my male colleagues had difficulty working for a woman with a nonhierarchical management style, they did not show it, or kept it to themselves.

I'm not sure why men appear to deal better with having a woman in charge, but I think I understand why it's sometimes difficult for women to work for other women. Most working women of my generation were accustomed to reporting to men and viewed males as the authority figures.

Perhaps the biggest lesson I had to learn at HHS was that not everybody shared my around-the-clock devotion to changing the world. What drove me did not necessarily drive everyone else. But I also discovered that people who seemed complacent in their work could be motivated by a cause they believed in.

During my years as head of the HHS Regional Office, one of the programs I developed that I was especially proud of was called the "Freedom from Fear" Campaign, designed to raise awareness of all kinds of family violence and encourage all people to take responsibility for stopping it. And we urged women to take control of their lives. Central to the program was information. That's usually the case. The more we know about something, including resources available to help, the less we have to fear and the better we'll be able to recognize and act on our best options.

Learning how to build a support system is pivotal to overcoming fear. My HHS Regional Office team worked to communicate through presentations, newsletters and other vehicles that people did not have to solve their problems alone. Regardless of how hard it is to believe, the big old lumbering government can actually help individual human beings and many programs exist to do that. I spoke often about "Freedom from Fear" to a wide range of audiences and had fascinating feedback. The most memorable and gratifying comment came from a man who told me that he knew his son was abusing his wife, and he vowed to confront him and stop the violence.

When I made the transition to HHS, I didn't want to compromise the important goal of change that characterized my life. I knew it was important for me to ask—and to answer—two questions right from day one:

- *When it came my time to move on, what did I want to be able to say I had accomplished?*
- *What did I want others, including the employees, to say about me and my tenure there?*

The answer to the first was easy. I wanted to make our delivery system for health care and social services better than it had been, friendlier and more accessible. I wanted to minimize the pain of government policy changes like welfare reform on the people affected, and to demonstrate resourcefulness through imagination and innovation.

The second question was a little more complicated. I wanted the civil servants in the regional office to think of me as more than a typical political appointee, a manager they admired or a person they liked. I wanted all of them, men and women, to view me as a strong, effective, and compassionate leader, who happened to be a woman.

When I left as HHS Regional Director, Secretary Shalala issued this statement, which read, in part, "On behalf of President Clinton, I want to thank Lynn for her outstanding service. She has left her mark as Regional Director, not only throughout the department, but on the broader national health and family agenda as well. Lynn has provided inspired leadership and dedicated service . . . (providing) the catalyst for 'Envisioning a Healthier Philadelphia,' a coalition . . . that seeks to form a more coordinated system of health and related social services for Philadelphia families.

She has also been instrumental in addressing the crisis of family violence, has been a leader on women's and family issues, and she spearheaded the raising of more than $2 million for charity . . . in her first year as Regional Director. We will certainly miss her, but we wish her well . . ."

When people ask me about purpose in life, I frequently tell them that what has motivated me is "absenteeism"—the absence of women from the tables of power, the absence of women from the circle of decision makers, and the absence of women from the list of architects blueprinting the future.

Women in the forefront of the quest for this kind of equality will remember just how burdensome the battle has been. Every woman who has marched in the street for a cause, risking ridicule and hostility, every woman who has been turned down for a job because "we need someone with more experience," every woman penalized financially and career-wise because of caregiving responsibilities—all of us have pride in the progress made and the emotional scars that go with it.

Increasing the numbers of women in positions of power has been glacial in its pace. Part of the reason it's been slow is that we take single examples and progressive acts as signs of the end-all solution. Upon seeing the headlines that one woman is seated in a chair at the head of the table where no women had ever been, we tend to ease up on the pressure and believe our work is done.

It is very easy to make peace with partial progress, to be fooled by the replacement of one "ism"—absenteeism—with another—tokenism.

But I believe that every woman in a high profile position in our society must be an inspiration for multiplication. Donna Shalala is one of those women, always helping other women and performing so well in her high visibility leadership roles. She and other trailblazing women have set the standards for women to now more routinely fill key positions of power in government. Frances Perkins would be gratified.

While part of my HHS agenda was to be an example and a source of encouragement for women, I also learned, on both a professional and personal level, about a special kind of fear that affects the older generation. My father died at almost ninety-two, just six months after I took that job. My mother would outlive him by eleven years and exemplify the "Fear of Aging" that was a visible outcome of an America that had learned to live much longer. The challenge is how to make those extra years worth the wait. We assembled some ideas that we thought would help.

CHAPTER 23

In Our Search for Who We Are,
Is It Useful to Return to Where We Came From?

Writer Judith Krantz said it. "A woman I graduated from college with told me plastic surgery was vulgar, that lines were a sign of character, that it's beautiful to age. I said 'Bull.' Character is internal. If you want to present yourself to the world with a face-lift, why the hell not? Many women approaching fifty don't feel glamorous; they feel invisible, but if they send out the right vibes, they won't be."

Politicians plead for their vote.

Pharmaceutical companies rely on them for black ink in the profit and loss column. Movie theaters offer them discounts.

Churches and gambling casinos send a bus to pick them up.

And a business called "Assisted Living" thrives on them, regardless of the state of the economy.

Although old age will always seem twenty years older than I am, there is no denying the influence on our society of an ever-growing segment of people who live a generation longer than we used to. I'm not sure when "old people" became "senior citizens," but during the twentieth century, medical science figured out how to keep us alive longer.

When that happened, a lot of years were added, but so were some unanticipated problems.

What do we do with the fourth generation?

Where will they live?

Who is supposed to take care of them?

How do we make their lives meaningful?

Will they bankrupt the Social Security system?

What do we do about the fears of elderly people?

I thought about all of those questions during my time at Health and Human Services in the final five years of the twentieth century. My interest was both professional, as I carried out my duties as Regional Director of the HHS Mid-Atlantic area, and personal, since my own parents had been destined to live into years that left them unable to care for themselves.

To address some of the issues, we at HHS in Philadelphia developed a program called "Aging Unafraid," a natural extension of our "Freedom from Fear" initiative. The object was to communicate as much helpful information as we could to seniors about how to cope with chronic illnesses, physical limitations, and the dread of loneliness, dependency, financial, and emotional stress, including the appalling possibility of abuse or neglect by their own family members.

The seeds of this program endured with me even after I left the Clinton administration in 2000. In work I would take on later with the Institute for Women's Health and Leadership at Drexel University College of Medicine, I had the opportunity to reach many in the aging population with messages about making those extra years healthier and happier.

One of my favorite octogenarians from history was Susan Brownell Anthony, known for her pioneering heroism as a champion of the struggle to win the right for women to vote in America. She died in 1906, fourteen years before the goal to which she had devoted her life was achieved, but her influence was significant.

One thing that fascinates me about her is that at a time when the life expectancy for a woman was forty-nine, she lived to be 86. And live she did.

"The older I get, the greater power I seem to have to help the world," she said. "I am like a snowball—the farther I am rolled, the more I gain."

Susan B. Anthony was the opposite personality from her suffragist colleague Elizabeth Cady Stanton. While Stanton relied on persuasion and charm, Anthony earned a reputation as one of the cause's most zealous and humorless advocates. She was a tireless worker, and if she didn't invent perseverance, she certainly exemplified it.

Newspapers ridiculing her campaign in New York for the liberalization of laws regarding married women's property heaped abuse on her. She won that fight in 1860.

Twelve years later at the age of fifty-two, which put her on overtime in life expectancy statistics, she cast a vote in the 1872 presidential election, in Rochester, New York.

That got her arrested, convicted and fined. One of history's legal footnotes records that the judge's directed verdict of guilty was written before the trial began. In one more exercise of her commitment, Susan B. Anthony refused to pay the fine, and the case was carried no further.

For the next thirty years she was actively engaged in her campaign for women's equality. With no guidelines for what she could do and could not do in her "golden years," she took over the presidency of the National American Woman Suffrage Association in 1892. She was seventy-two.

The message from her later years ought to guide us now—that senior citizens care about the same issues as all other ages, because they've already been *all other ages*. That's what makes them valuable. They have experience.

Contrary to social policy and tradition, people do not turn sixty-five and automatically shut down their brainpower. Nor their sense of responsibility. Nor their beauty. As far back as 1852 Harriet Beecher Stowe wrote: "So much has been said and sung of beautiful young girls. Why doesn't someone wake up to the beauty of old women?"

Accomplishment is not the sole property of the fifty-nine-and-under crowd.

At sixty, Ruth Bader Ginsburg was named to the U.S. Supreme Court.

At sixty-three, Agatha Christie wrote *The Mousetrap*, which became the world's longest-running play.

At sixty-five, Elizabeth Hazen discovered nystatin for the treatment of life-threatening diseases.

At sixty-six, Maggie Kuhn founded the Gray Panthers.

At seventy, Golda Meir was elected Prime Minister of Israel.

At seventy-seven, Louise Nevelson designed the interior of the Chapel of the Good Shepherd in St. Peter's Church in New York.

At eighty-one, Barbara McClintock won the Nobel Prize for Physiology for her revolutionary work in genetics.

At eighty-seven, Jeanette Rankin, the first woman to serve in Congress, led an anti-Vietnam war rally on Capitol Hill.

At ninety-five, Martha Graham premiered her latest choreographed work, "Maple Leaf Gala."

Achievers know what time it is and what day it is, but they forget how old they are. In her book, *Outrageous Acts and Everyday Rebellions*, Gloria Steinem wrote:

"Women may be the one group that grows more radical with age." In May of 2009, I attended Gloria's seventy-fifth birthday celebration at the Ms. Foundation's annual dinner in New York, and she was as beautiful—and radical—as ever.

Finding both challenge and contentment in the final chapter of one's life was never meant to be an easy assignment. Whoever said "old age is not for sissies" nailed it. I experienced the uncomfortable intimacy of watching close-up the final years of my father and mother.

Both spent their last decades in a fine facility of their own personal choosing that enabled them to transition from independence to total dependence, but their lives were circumscribed and lacking in joy from my point of view.

Their physical capacity was limited, their mental agility there to the end.

It was excruciatingly painful to watch the man who worked his Virginia farm, who ran a business, who served vigorously in the halls of America's highest legislative body, who led a fundraising campaign to establish the Eastern Virginia Medical School, who was a leader in his community and his country, lose his sight and his mobility. When he could no longer drive, his fiery independence was permanently wounded.

My mother's final years were even more difficult to witness because they dragged on. She suffered from Parkinson's disease, lost her sight and her hearing, and worst of all, her cherished dignity.

True to their principles, both my parents died as bravely as they had lived, clinging to their Christian faith until the end. They did not want to move in with me and my family, reasoning unselfishly that they had lived their lives and I should be free to live mine. There was no guilt conveyed in that decision, and it was a great gift to me.

One of the realities of people living longer is the evolution of the four-generation family. The "sandwich generation," having already raised their own children, must decide whether they will care for their aging parents or help with their grandchildren.

All six of my grandchildren were born during the eleven years between my parents' deaths, and I felt torn between helping with my mother's needs and my children's growing responsibilities.

Depending on the longevity of the middle generation, little of one's life span may be free of caregiving.

Each family makes its own choices. "Aging unafraid" involves more people than just the one doing the aging.

Family is a depository where you bank a wide selection of emotions—love, loyalty, and unity have to make room in the account for some portions of anger, envy and rebellion. The fiber of a family gets tested often, and the way we handle those exams determines the strength of a family's continuity.

A close examination of most families will probably reveal a strong interest for each generation to set financial goals that will help their children live better than they did in their time. What doesn't get as much attention is a parallel concentration on helping each new generation to live better in terms of honesty, compassion, respect, commitment, unselfishness.

Making a living dominates our energy. Making a life gets second billing.

So many of the major events in our lives are shaped by the lessons learned in the family classroom. Some actions are spurred by an urge to meet expectations handed down by the generations. Others happen as a direct form of resistance to those expectations.

I went to the college my parents chose to meet those expectations.

I went to Europe to resist them.

I married well and had two wonderful children after watching my parents do the same.

I pursued a life of independent advocacy for women to achieve equal footing, in or out of marriage, concluding the conventional role of "the wife" restricted women from discovering their potential.

I ran for the U.S. Senate because I had learned from my family to serve others and to do what I felt was right.

I harbored guilt for the time away from home that my "change" ambitions required.

Family pushes and pulls. It's a tug-of-war. Its evolution over the past century has empowered women with freedom while at the same time saddling them with obligation.

That where we came from, and what happened to us while we were there, influences the decisions we make about our own lives seems undeniable. It's what we do with that knowledge that determines how meaningful our lives will be.

For women the tension is real. While being a majority of the population, we still settle for a minority of the available power. While wanting to be respected for leadership and decision making, many sacrifice that admiration to be told they are good mothers. While wanting the approval of the board of directors for a strategic plan, some place greater value on praise from the family at Thanksgiving for a successful dinner.

We're learning, slowly and with some degree of pain, that the choices women make do not come with a "happy ever after" warranty. But one thing is becoming more clear—they are our choices.

For most of life's turning points, the family provides continuity. I like Elizabeth Stone's comment in her book *Black Sheep and Kissing Cousins*. She writes, "Like all cultures, one of the family's first jobs is to persuade its members they're special, more wonderful than the neighboring barbarians." Now we're back to love, loyalty, unity—the best parts of any family.

CHAPTER 24

Why Is Decision Making So Difficult, So Demanding, So Irresistible?

Spreading self-doubt among women is a growth business. Magazines at the hairdresser's carry articles like "The Chronically Single Woman," intending to strike fear into the hearts of those who portray "getting a man" as an essential merit badge in a woman's quest for a life of value. Television commercials shame women who are carrying an extra ounce on their hips, who are using the wrong shampoo, or whose facial wrinkles are showing. In a world of males and females, whatever it is that's hitting the fan is not being evenly distributed.

The reason I've become so persistent about women exercising power over our own lives is the basic argument for equality: only those who bear the consequences of a decision have a right to make it.

Historically, my principal quarrel with decisions that have limited women's choices and opportunities has been not only with the men who issued those edicts, but with the women who stood by passively and accepted whatever results accompanied those decisions.

I believe that our ability to solve the puzzle of a woman's life will be determined by how quickly we find the corner pieces—the fundamentals of our own independence.

Beyond marriage and children and getting an education I could rely on, there have been four major phases of my public service life. All of them involved decision making that I reserved for myself. I have never wanted others to decide how I was going to live.

In phase 1, I made a decision that I had more to offer and explore than going for the *Good Housekeeping* gold. I've never second-guessed anyone who enjoys homemaking. In fact, I envy good cooks. But my early personal experience with gender discrimination, and a natural inclination to lead, resulted in my directing my energies outward, toward achieving fairness for women. That led to two active decades with CHOICE, the Family Planning Council, Women's Way, and the Junior League, among other community commitments, and seeking a public platform for expressing my beliefs.

In phase 2, I made the decision to run for the U.S. Senate after Anita Hill had taken so much heat from an all-male group of senators during the Clarence Thomas hearings. That decision was made with an understanding that there would be consequences—objections of my family, loss of privacy, attacks by a win-or-else opponent. The truth was that the positive aspects of that all-consuming campaign would far surpass the downside, but it took a while for me to see that. I believed it was time for women to claim what was two centuries overdue. Later, with a sense of unfinished business, I tried two more times to get elected to public office. Though, in hindsight and for a variety of reasons, they were not the best decisions, they had one thing in common with my 1992 experience—they were my decisions.

During phase 3, I took my public service aspirations "inside the system" and worked from there, instead of my customary stance of raising hell from the outside. My time as a regional director of Health and Human Services for the federal government helped me to focus not only on the problems of women of all ages, but on the entire family. Those years confirmed for me that with the right system and the right spirit, the nation's government can and *must* deliver on the promise its founders articulated so eloquently.

My major phase 4 decision was to take what I had learned about getting things done and accept a position where my experience could bring added value to an academic institution with a unique history of trailblazing women and values aligned with mine. Joining Drexel University College of Medicine was an unexpected opportunity. I was hired as director of the "Institute for Women's Health and Leadership." The name alone captured my life's work and purpose—women's health, in all its physical and emotional scope, and women's leadership, in all its exciting and evolving stages. Accepting responsibilities that had academic underpinnings in an institution that encouraged innovation was one of those "just right" choices.

These four major decisions were validated by many supplementary ones along the way, but when I pause to reflect, I find that without really planning to do so, I made an orderly transition. Any turbulence that came with it was intentional.

A cumulative result of my career path has been the development of "Lynn's Laws"—six suggestions I will give my grandchildren if they ask, and probably even if they don't.

Law Number 1: *Do not outsource your decisions.*
    Part of grasping the realization of power is having the will to use it. Call on people you trust for advice if you'd like. An extra set of brains is usually helpful, but remember you are the writer, producer, director, and star of your life story. Avoid delegating the important decisions to others. The fun is in the choices you make yourself, good and not-so-good.

Law Number 2: *Don't be afraid to find out what's behind Door No. 3.*
    What makes life full are the risks that come with it. If you start every day determined not to run the risk of being embarrassed or hurt, you may live your life shielded from disappointment but you will also miss exciting new discoveries and block your view of a better tomorrow. Almost everything new that I've tried has been accompanied by butterflies, but once you get them flying in formation, you can soar with them.

Law Number 3: *Don't settle for Marvin Gardens.*
    When you're thinking out a decision, give the possibilities more attention than the problems. People who approach a new venture with an overload of reasons not to do it are more vulnerable to the temptation of playing it safe. Weigh the obstacles, yes, but not without equal or more emphasis on the potential. I never looked at a new opportunity or job as a rigid set of requirements. I preferred to look and see if what exists is a base from which I can make the opportunity grow. In the game of Monopoly, if you land on Marvin Gardens, don't forget that Boardwalk and Park Place are just a little farther down the board.

Law Number 4: *Don't wait until everything is "just right."*
    In most of the challenging choices of life, delay itself is a decision. Time for thought is okay, but if you hesitate in order to build a consensus among all around you, the best result may be an outcome where you can share the blame. Worrying about what others will think is probably relying excessively on the theory that

they really care that much anyway. It is your life, your decision, and if everything is not "just right," remember you can make it right when you get there.

Law Number 5: *Don't lose sight of the invisible.*

In a perfect world, the decision you're about to make will have a positive impact on the lives of others. You do not take on a new adventure in your life without the probability that you will have passengers on the trip. If what you are about to do has the potential to inspire a dozen, a hundred, a thousand other people—that is something to be factored into your personal decision-making process. It may be fashionable to ask "*What will happen if I do nothing?*" But it is just as appropriate to ask "*What won't happen if I do nothing?*" Somehow I get the sense that Elizabeth Cady Stanton and Susan B. Anthony asked themselves that question.

Law Number 6: *Don't dismiss your role in history.*

Because women have had to swim against the current ever since Adam blamed Eve for a downturn in the apple industry, we have been taught to be spectators to what's happening around us, often sitting on the curb and watching the parade go by. Women have been allowed to read all of history, but to make very little of it. That changes every time we make an important decision of our own. One woman's decisiveness strengthens another's. It's a wonderfully contagious contribution to that part of the "History of Women" that is still unwritten, and every woman, by her actions, can be her own author.

I once heard a speaker say: "I was going to talk about being decisive . . . but I changed my mind."

If there was a "Lynn's Law Number 7," it would deal with the very legitimate tactic of changing your course of action if you find that it simply isn't working. That, too, is a decision.

I like decision making. I'm most comfortable with leadership responsibility, while understanding that being in the spotlight is certain to draw criticism. I've learned that even some who benefit from a battle won may eventually turn on you.

My enthusiasm for stirring things up had an early beginning. When I was seven years old, my maternal grandfather nicknamed me "the agitator." He was referring to my role as the organizer/ringleader of my cousins' activities and he said it with a mixture of scolding and amused approval.

On one count, I believe it's something I have to do in order to advance a cause I feel is right. On the other hand, at times it's painful to be a lightning rod—perceived as controversial, knowing that my motives are being criticized and questioned.

But criticism and doubt are not adequate reasons for taking yourself out of the game.

In 1992, Eleanor Davis, then in her midfifties, climbed with others to the summit of Mt. Kilimanjaro. Two years later she and her team reached the top of Mt. Rainier.

She was a breast cancer survivor and scaled the peaks to raise money for breast cancer research, and to prove she could do it.

She said of her decision: "Climbing a mountain is not easy. Each time I say to myself, 'Oh, God, why am I doing this?' It's wet and cold. You go without a bath for ten days. You get sick of drinking iodine water. Near the top, you can't breathe and your head is dizzy and your heart is flipping over.

"But the sense of accomplishment from forcing your body to its limits is exhilarating. You have to dig down real deep to find the extra energy and spirit to keep going.

"Everyone has a different Everest. You gain strength, courage, and confidence by every experience in which you really stop to look fear in the face. You are able to say 'I lived through this. I can take the next thing that comes along.'"

Day-to-day decision making, large and small, does not require the physical daring of mountain climbing, but when those decisions are about how you want to live your life, they are best not left for others to make.

Many decisions in life are seat-of-the-pants choices. Some women say yes to marriage proposals in light so dim you wouldn't buy a dress by it.

Many choices are based on intuition. I've been asked if I believe in intuition. Believe in it? I rely on it.

But intuition works better when it's backed up by judgment honed over the years. Most of my decisions have been the result of cumulative wisdom based on all the good and bad that has happened to me.

I had seen that it was possible to get the public's attention to the needs of women, and when the offer came to head the Institute for Women's Health and Leadership, I felt the horizon widening. The proud history of women in medicine was a foundation to be built upon.

Still, this meant academia. I didn't have the academic credentials of my predecessors or colleagues. And I'm not good with hierarchy. But the three magic words in plain view were *women, health, leadership*. Those words resonated. This decision was "go."

CHAPTER 25

Is Truth Closer When We Ask All the Questions, Even Though We May Not Like the Answers?

Winning acceptance of anything new and different depends on convincing people that "new" is better than "old," that change is better than more of the same. Pioneers going west did not stop at the Mississippi River. They found a way to cross it, later to bridge it, and then to fly over it. Edna Ferber wrote: "I am not belittling brave men, but the sunbonnet as well as the sombrero has helped to settle this glorious land of ours." That probably should be said often because with communication comes awareness—and for women, awareness can mean a fresh start, maybe even a longer life.

Curiosity is invincible.

To quote Eleanor Roosevelt: "I think, at a child's birth, if a mother could ask a fairy godmother to endow the child with the most useful gift, that gift should be curiosity."

When I accepted the invitation to become director of the Institute for Women's Health and Leadership at Drexel University College of Medicine, it did not take long to sense an opportunity to create a delivery system for information that could increase women's knowledge about their own health—physical and mental. It also did not take long to recognize the connection between more women in leadership and science and advances in women's health.

Our mission and our audience were pretty well summed up by a simple statement of purpose we developed—"Helping women everywhere live healthier and more fulfilling lives."

One of the benefits of my career with its series of distinct episodes has been the overlap of acquaintances—those connecting dots in the pursuit of a useful life.

Dr. Glenda Donoghue was director of the Institute when I met her during my tenure with the Department of Health and Human Services.

The Institute was one of the first six National Centers of Excellence in Women's Health designated by DHHS, and I was proud to have it and two others of the original six—50 percent!—in my Mid-Atlantic region.

Glenda invited me to a ribbon-cutting ceremony at what was called "the Gatehouse," an old structure on the historic campus of the Medical College of Pennsylvania in Philadelphia. Previously a stable, a classroom, and a restaurant, the Gatehouse was to be the home of the Institute; and on my visit I became fascinated by exhibits from the College of Medicine's archives depicting the early years of women becoming physicians despite fierce resistance by "the medical establishment" at the time. I learned that this medical school traced its origins to 1850, when the Female Medical College of Pennsylvania was founded as the first medical school for women.

From Glenda I inherited the Institute's remarkable substance when I arrived. Already in place were a Women's Health Education Program and a Center for Women's Health, the first incorporating state-of-the-art knowledge of women's health in the medical education curricula, and the second providing innovative primary care with a holistic approach to each patient, recognizing the "cradle-to-grave" continuum of women's unique health needs. As the Center's Director, Dr. Katherine Sherif, said, "This is not 'bikini medicine.' We're focused on all the body parts."

One of the Institute's premier programs then and now is ELAM, an acronym for Executive Leadership in Academic Medicine Program for Women. It attracts women from all over the United States and Canada, from medical, dental, and public health schools, whose goals and credentials identify them as potential leaders in their fields. ELAM is an intensive yearlong program whose graduates fill some of the most visible senior positions at academic and other health centers in the United States.

I like being around people who make me smarter by the force of their intellect and the level of their devotion to their life's work. I met many of those at Drexel University College of Medicine. I found accord with some, disagreements with others, and valuable leadership lessons from all.

Occasionally, I still wonder why I was chosen as Director of the Institute, which included the coveted title of Betty A. Cohen Chair in Women's Health. I am not a doctor. I do not have a string of degrees to enhance my "curriculum vitae." I believe that several things may have worked for me—my identification with women's issues, my willingness to lead, my connections, and my success in raising money. These were all assets that could benefit this high-potential program.

The fundraising resourcefulness would be tested often, but nowhere more pressured than in raising money for those archival treasures inherited by Drexel from the long history of its predecessor medical schools (the second being Hahnemann which was founded in 1848). The Archives and Special Collections on Women in Medicine and Homeopathy were moved into the Institute soon after I arrived and this became one of my greatest challenges.

In the midst of previous organizational dance steps, the memories and mementos of a century-and-a-half had become nomads, wandering in the wilderness of high-stakes corporate mergers and bankruptcies. It would have been easy for what was arguably the most important collection of information on the gallant history of women in medicine to simply disintegrate from neglect.

The Institute became the guardian of the legacy, particularly that of the all-female medical school that was founded in the nineteenth century because medical colleges at that time either rejected women applicants or marginalized the few who were brave enough to enroll.

A woman studying medicine in the 1850s was an oddity. She wasn't to be taken seriously, and if she did become a doctor, chances were that she would have a hard time establishing a medical practice. Some women physicians went to faraway lands to work with people who had diseases we did not know how to cure—and, sadly, often died from those very diseases.

To this day I find their story an inspiration in the uphill climb of American women. What happened to women in medicine—the abuse they took and indignities they refused to endure—ought to be taught to every girl in every school in the land. Medicine is one of the few professions where women have caught up numerically in terms of education. Half of all medical students are now female, but the percentage of women in medical leadership remains small.

Concerned that pieces of a valuable history were poorly housed in multiple storage areas where they were inaccessible to researchers and scholars, and that a treasure of important research material was endangered, Joanne Murray, the Archives director, made a compelling case for the urgency of the need for a new and permanent home for the collections.

That's where my role as fundraiser came in. Drexel decided in 2008 to build a wing to house the Institute on the medical school campus at Queen Lane in Philadelphia, an idea recommended by my team. We petitioned the university to add a floor where the Legacy Center could be located in a permanent home. We received a conditional okay. It would be built if we could raise a lot of money on a tight time schedule. We went to work immediately. The Legacy Center is now a high-tech resource for researchers and scholars all over the world.

Pivotal to our fundraising success, and to most programs at the Institute is D. Walter Cohen, D.D.S., Chancellor Emeritus of the College of Medicine. I had met him years earlier when he presented to me the MCP/Gimbel Award, at that time among the most prestigious honors for a woman in Philadelphia. I was humbled and gratified to be chosen that year and delighted to get to know Dr. Cohen.

Walter believes in women's health and leadership. He is the founder of the ELAM Program and established the Betty A. Cohen Chair in Women's Health, the first endowed chair of its kind, in honor of his late wife. He is a world-renowned periodontist, an academic and civic leader, a productive fundraiser, and a thoroughly decent human being with both a sense of purpose and a sense of humor. In his eighties, he is the youngest man I know.

Conversations with Walter about the absence of an award in Philadelphia for extraordinary women (the MCP/Gimbel Award had been discontinued) led to the establishment of a classic program that illustrates the mobilizing value of innovative communications. We named it "WOMAN ONE." It is an annual program, each year celebrating the leadership of an outstanding woman.

WOMAN ONE has a second purpose, to raise money for scholarships for underrepresented minority women who aspire to become physicians. This unique idea resulted from declining applications from minorities and increasing tuition costs for medical school. WOMAN ONE scholars all have inspiring stories of their own, and as they graduate and go to on practice medicine in underserved areas, the value of this good idea keeps multiplying.

The question with which I regularly challenged my staff in the early days at the Institute was—"How do we bring about positive change for the greatest number of women in America?"

So many American women and children live in communities that are underserved medically. It makes sense that good healthcare enables good education which in turn generates better opportunities in life. The opposite side of the equation is that poor healthcare stymies the pursuit of education and dooms generation after generation to substandard lifestyles. The result is that girls growing into women never discover their true potential.

One answer, it seemed, was to build the inventory of talented and committed minority women in the medical profession by supporting young women with the brainpower and motivation to become physicians who are interested in practicing medicine in disadvantaged areas.

In a normal year a doctor may treat four thousand patients. Multiply that by an average forty-year career and the numbers grow to six figures. Then multiply that by the number of new physicians we could fund and we're talking about millions of people touched by our scholars.

Our family of WOMAN ONE honorees and scholars developed a special admiration for each other, and the more senior medical students helped and encouraged the newer ones. The program became a unique success that continues to give me great pride. By the end of its seventh year, fifteen WOMAN ONE scholars had received a total of $500,000 in tuition support. Five of those had graduated and were practicing medicine in underserved communities.

From the beginning, the annual award ceremony was different. We were determined to be audience-friendly. No sit-down dinner, no speechmaking, plenty of changes of pace. Some music, laughs, surprises, and wonderful award winners including TV personality Suzanne Roberts, Olympic basketball star Dawn Staley, and renowned horticulturalist Jane Pepper. We wanted WOMAN ONE to communicate the remarkable contributions of women leaders and the promise of a new wave of young physicians.

Another communications delivery system for the Institute that I introduced gained immediate popularity. Understanding the need to reach women with information they could use about good health practices, we presented "Conversations about Women's Health." I am not one who believes that the problems of the world can be solved by another seminar, but I am an advocate of face-to-face exchanges of knowledge between those who have it and those who need it.

"Conversations"—in neighborhoods, churches, schools, and senior citizen centers—worked so well that I wanted to extend them to the topic of women's leadership. My time to do that on a larger stage was coming.

CHAPTER 26

Will We Ever Act Like the Majority We Are?

In May 2000, I went to Washington to be a part of the Million Mom March. I had participated in marches before, but this one with its focus on handgun control was massive. It reminded me of just how well women can mobilize when we join forces. Anna Quindlen, one of the speakers, asked the assembled crowd to contact members of Congress and urge them to support gun control. She said, "When they ask why, tell them the same thing you tell your children—because I said so!" Skeptics later asked what was accomplished that day. I believe we proved that women of all ages, races, and religions are capable of great unity when we get angry enough. A decade later there are still plenty of reasons for that anger.

The "Conversations about Women's Health" that we presented at Drexel's Institute for Women's Health and Leadership caught on with the public in a hurry because the information was packaged in an easy-to-absorb fashion.

We knew that women often neglected their own health. They still do. Some put off checking with the doctor because they can't afford it, and many are so busy taking care of others in the family that they just don't get around to addressing their own needs. (I'm counting on the 2010 health insurance reform law to eliminate the first reason.)

We knew those women were overlooking the fact that as the prime caregivers—an assignment handed to us by nature, tradition and default—we do no favor for those we care for by permitting our own health to go downhill. I often use the analogy of the flight attendant's instruction as the plane prepares to take off—"Put on your own oxygen mask first before assisting others."

At the Institute, we were determined to carry the message to our audiences live and in person. We knew that the general public, given all the options available for spending discretionary hours, wasn't likely to sit still for lectures and wouldn't warm up to brochures filled with medical terms.

For each conversation, we lined up three or four experts, usually doctors, on the topic we were discussing. It might be heart disease or diabetes, sex, alcohol and drugs, or depression.

Typically, when people walk into a room that has three people sitting behind a table on stage and a moderator at a podium, it's predictable that each panelist will speak for ten to fifteen minutes before responding to questions from those in the audience still awake at that time.

We decided to change all that to match the sound bite system—what I call the "*USA Today* approach"—by which people now get much of their information in the twenty-first century. No warm up. No preliminary comments. Within the first thirty seconds, members of the panel were giving brief answers to specific questions.

I moderated these conversations because (a) somebody had to, (b) I had tried the approach successfully during my years at the Department of Health and Human Services, (c) I wanted to illustrate to my staff how important I thought these sessions were, and (d) I really enjoyed bridging the communication gap between the specialists and the public who needed the information. In a sense, I felt like the translator.

The panelists were asked to deliver short, direct answers. We had told them no preparation was required. Their life's work was all the rehearsal necessary. We called this a BYOB event—Bring Your Own Brain.

One Saturday morning we presented a conversation for teenage girls and their mothers. My opening question to the panel was—"What were you doing when you were thirteen?" One of the panelists instantly got the audience's attention by replying, "I had a baby."

So much of communicating effectively depends upon a no-frills approach to delivering information. Our success with the conversation format has thrived on giving people information they can understand and use. It depends on women in the audience feeling comfortable enough to ask any question they may have. Once they get the answers they need, they are able to start leading healthier lives because they have more confidence in their own judgment. We also learned, from notes and calls I received following some of these programs, that we were opening up dialogue among family members on important health topics they had previously been reluctant to discuss.

Good communication among women can propel us to where we ought to be. We can help each other solve the puzzle of why we, as a majority, continue to accept the minority label.

According to the U.S. Census Bureau, there are 148 million males in the country, and 152 million females. I see it as our collective responsibility to use our voices, views, and values, so long relegated to "women's issues," on wider concerns.

After all, who decided that our influence on economic policy should be limited or nonexistent, with those decisions best left to men?

Who decided that we are less equipped to deal with terrorists and a turbulent world that could benefit from fresh minds that value peace over violence?

Who decided that we cannot bring to the boardroom the best ideas for products and services, especially considering that women are the vast majority of decision-making consumers?

To get motivated, we need to remind ourselves of these four principles.

- Though the future can come in all shapes and sizes, until women insist on contributing in a meaningful way, that future is going to be made up of the same problems we have right now.
- Women's influence on the world will be as big as we're united to make it. To grow that influence, we have to be more interested in what we're *about* to do than what we've *already* done.
- No one has a monopoly on integrity. Honesty is not a gender issue, but women are pretty good at it. A clear conscience is a soft pillow, and it will be even more comfortable if we become the leaders who exercise integrity, rather than the onlookers who hope others will behave better.
- Ending our imposed inferiority complex is an achievable goal. It can be done by individual declarations of independence, but it will happen sooner if we claim our interdependence and take our majority status seriously.

There are things we know and things we don't know.

We know that it took 144 years for women to win the right to vote. What we don't know is why nearly half of all eligible women squander that privilege by staying home on election day.

We know that more and more women are running for public office. What we don't know is why we are still coming up short in the House and Senate of the U.S. Congress and actually declining in number in state legislatures.

We know that for every man whose achievements we admire, there is a woman who also deserves our applause. What we don't know is why we are so reluctant to give her a standing ovation.

I cheer the aviation exploits of Charles Lindbergh, but my voice is just as loud in praise of Amelia Earhart.

I listen intently to the voice of James Earl Jones, but recalling the sounds of Barbara Jordan stirs more emotional juices in me.

I am amazed at the genius of Bill Gates, but also awed by the breakthrough made by Elizabeth Blackwell in becoming the first American woman physician, despite almost endless obstacles placed in her path.

In a world with equal rules, you can see the possibilities.

The Irving Berlin musical *Annie Get Your Gun* had a song called "Anything You Can Do, I Can Do Better." There is a charming competitive challenge between the sexes in the lyrics. It's too bad that so many women have to wait for misfortune in the lives of men in order to prove their own capability.

I think of Elizabeth Griscom and Margaret Madeline Chase.

Elizabeth was born in Philadelphia. Urged to "marry a good man" early, she did so at twenty-one. Her husband ran an upholstery business, which he had founded, but died three years after their marriage. Elizabeth, at the age of twenty-four, stepped in and took over the business.

In the next sixty years, she outlived two more husbands and turned the upholstery enterprise into a very profitable endeavor. She eventually left the business to her daughter with complete confidence, because Elizabeth had prepared her with the necessary leadership training.

History knows Elizabeth better for her connections with a U.S. president, and by her nickname "Betsy" that her first husband, John Ross, used to call her.

Although American history sings the praises of Betsy Ross for creating the new nation's flag, women need to be aware that Elizabeth Griscom did more than stitch and sew stars and stripes. She ran a successful business for nearly her entire lifetime.

Margaret Madeline Chase was twenty-three when she married newspaperman Clyde Smith. He dabbled in local politics and was elected to Congress. She went to Washington with him as his secretary. Four years later, and only ten years into their marriage, he died, and the people of her state elected Margaret to take his place.

Maine's Margaret Chase Smith served eight years in the House, four full terms in the Senate and distinguished herself so competently that *Newsweek* magazine named her Most Valuable Senator for 1960.

Her strength was her independence. In 1948 she pushed through passage of legislation that gave women in the military equal pay, rank, and privileges. She was an early opponent of fellow Republican Joseph McCarthy when the Wisconsin senator went on his reckless campaign to brand many Americans with a communist label.

Elizabeth Griscom and Margaret Madeline Chase were born a century-and-a-half apart, but their lives shared a condition that took a long time to change. They both had to wait for the unexpected deaths of their husbands in order to prove their own competence.

When I mention the Margaret Chase Smith story, sometimes my Democratic friends ask why I cite her as an example, since she was a Republican. While it's true that I'm a lifelong Democrat, I have many Republican friends, some of whom voted for me in my 1992 run for the U.S. Senate. I admire achievement, regardless of political affiliation.

I'm not much for labels. They seldom fit. Most people call me a liberal. My friends call me a progressive. Those who really know me don't apply labels.

From the beginning, my life goals had very little to do with political party affiliation. Those goals, all three of them, were concerned with helping women to achieve.

- To achieve freedom from fear of all types—violence, poverty, isolation, dependence, and discrimination.
- To achieve access to power by using our economic clout to support causes and candidates that reflect our values.
- To achieve equality of opportunity in education and employment, and never to be denied the right to make our own decisions about our reproductive lives.

In May of 2009, the Junior League of Philadelphia, where I had been president thirty years earlier, presented me with an award for my service to women. As I sat there listening to remarks that were far too flattering, but greatly appreciated, I quietly tried to grade my own report card on my goals of freedom from fear, access to power, equality of opportunity. How well have I succeeded in helping women toward those goals?

I came up with the only appropriate grade. I gave myself an *Incomplete*. As I accepted the award, I was pleased to be commended for motivating a certain awareness among many women but sobered by all the catching up that was still to be done.

CHAPTER 27

Dick and Jane. Jack and Jill.
Romeo and Juliet. Does First Billing Matter?

What does a woman learn when she comes home after an exhausting day at work and is greeted by a loving embrace from a partner, warm respect from children, and a problem-free, completely harmonious home? What she learns, of course, is that she's in the wrong place!

As we age, an inevitable pastime emerges and we look back to try to identify those people in our past who made the biggest differences in our lives, the ones who delivered flashes of illumination that launched us toward becoming the successes we are.

I've had some good teachers and mentors, women and men, at various stages of my life, and their encouragement and support at critical points helped me decide which fork in the road to take.

My favorite teacher in college was Dr. Robert Cornett, Professor of Philosophy. His provocative lectures about the Greeks like Plato and Socrates and subsequent philosophers who struggled with the meaning of life stimulated my critical thinking.

Two lasting fundamentals from my sixteen-plus years in structured study have thankfully stayed with me, and I'm grateful for their retention.

One was the nourishment of my interest in reading, especially staying abreast of current events. Early on, I absorbed the wisdom that "if you can't read, you can't lead." And that if you can read, and you don't, you are illiterate by choice.

To me reading is an essential source of knowledge. It is research. It is entertainment. It's aerobics for the brain. I've never known a creative writer who wasn't also a creative reader.

Newspapers, magazines, fiction, biographies, poetry. Bring it on. I seldom finish reading a page or a paragraph without gaining a new idea.

There was a second fundamental that my schooling helped to reinforce. That was my respect for the rights of others and my sense of obligation to help protect those rights when they were being denied.

The lessons in respect came first from home and then every Sunday when I went to church. But it was in school where the lessons found a laboratory, where the rules of behavior were tested every day.

You don't know about it in the early grades, or maybe you just don't think about it, but what's going on in the schoolyard is what's ahead in life. Some people are going to be in wonderful harmony with the way you think and act; and others will resist, resent, and reject you and your ideas.

Learning how to deal reasonably and intelligently with both is a course not yet taught in our educational system. I concede there must be value in memorizing dates, state capitals, and Asian mountain ranges; but I would have preferred, in place of focusing on the past, to have had equal emphasis on what was possible in the future. Imagination needs watering and weeding.

One of my joys in going to Drexel's Institute for Women's Health and Leadership was to look around at this intersection of academia and medicine and see so much of what I had always hoped to—busy professional women engaged in work of great worth, standing up for their points of view, constantly learning and on the alert for new challenges.

The chicken and the egg question doesn't bother me. It doesn't matter whether education made these women more conscious of their value, or the women made education more responsive to their interests. As long as it's happening, the atmosphere of respect for women inches a little further up the ladder.

Though I tried not to show it, during the first few months in my academic surroundings at the Institute, I struggled to figure out where and how I fit in. In my three-part career to date, I had been in the living-on-a-shoestring nonprofit world where the cause overruled caution, in the rough-and-tumble mud wrestling environment of political campaigns, and in the structured routine sameness of governmental bureaucracy where disruptions were mostly of my own making.

In this new setting, my colleagues were swimming in degrees and published papers. I've earned two degrees, my Bachelor of Arts and a late-in-life Master of Science in Management mostly to add a few more initials behind my name. At the Institute I was a generalist in a world of specialists. I had to remind myself of what I was good at—advocating for women, building teams, getting things done, raising money, and connecting people who have resources to the people who need them in order to improve opportunities for women.

The Institute was better known nationally in academic circles than it was locally. My new colleagues' words of purpose upon my arrival remained with me. They said, "We want you to give us a higher profile in the community."

It was another lesson in how a well-assembled coalition works best. Each person uses his or her talents to complement the contribution of the rest of the team.

That, too, is something I never had in school—the course on teamwork.

Most of our lives are guided by a series of teams. We are born through a team of mother, father, doctor, nurse, and health insurance agent. We are educated by a team of teachers. If we're in sports, or the chorus, or some other extracurricular activity, we become part of a team and may even get uniforms so we all look alike.

If we go to work, it's usually in a group setting. If we get married, there's another team—bride, groom, presiding official, photographer, caterer.

Even when we die, in many cases we are carried by a team of six pallbearers.

There would seem to be some logic in the thought that if most of our life is going to involve working in "teams," some formal instruction on the basics of teamwork ought to be taught, instead of having to learn it in Realityland.

The course content seems pretty clear. I envision about a dozen subjects with titles like Cooperation, Unselfishness, Trust, Integrity, Loyalty, Time Management, Goal Setting, Understanding, Evaluation, Conflict Resolution, Credit Sharing, and Leadership.

Teach that in the fifth grade and every year until young people get out of college, and postgraduate work will come with their first job.

We don't teach leadership in our early education system. Leaders tend to emerge by the sheer force of their personalities, as a result of special talent, or by the unwillingness of other people to take charge. I'm not sure what combination of these two conditions pushed me into so many leadership roles, but I've learned that if I'm on the team, I want to lead it. The Myers-Briggs test of personality traits summed me up when the results showed that I cannot *not* lead.

I'm not sure if my inclination to be chair of every meeting started because of my family background or in spite of it.

Each of us begins with a family of chance and moves on to a family of choice. We cannot control the circumstances of our birth—not our gender, race, or national origin. But as life moves along, we form a family of choice. In a free society, we select our friends, our sexual partners, our workplace associates, and decide when and whether to have children.

It is in those relationships with our "family of choice" that we have the best chance to improve the world we inhabit. Women, caught in the undertow of discrimination for so long, can create significant change because there is so much ground to make up. History has provided men with a huge lead in the gender competition. In order to catch up, women have to rely on ourselves to establish new standards and models of personal and public behavior.

Those lessons I learned in an all-girls' school and an all-women college.

One by one, those institutions are disappearing from the American educational scene. It's particularly true of the all-female colleges.

Two recent examples of those victims of economic pressure were close enough to me to hurt when it happened, when the announcement that they were going co-ed was released, through clenched teeth.

One was Rosemont College, where I had made the 1992 commencement address amid vigorous protest from some Catholic leaders about my stand on women's reproductive rights.

Seventeen years later I was on an airplane next to a prominent local news anchor and lifelong Rosemont College devotee. The "going coed" decision had just been made, for financial reasons. You could feel the pain in her voice. She had a passion in her heart for the college and a vivid awareness that education at an all-women's college is an experience to be valued.

I felt the same way. I shared with her that my college, Randolph-Macon Woman's College, had also decided to admit men and that the move had upset me, my four cousins who had attended the school and a large number of other alumnae.

I feel the intensity of their allegiance. Impressive statistics demonstrate that women of my generation who were educated at all-female institutions are much more likely to be found in significant leadership roles than those who graduated from coed colleges.

At the Institute for Women's Health and Leadership we were doing some educating of our own, through our system of conversations with women in the community. So many of these discussions kept coming back to the need for more women in leadership positions.

With the year 2020 not too far distant, and the centennial of the suffrage amendment waiting to be celebrated, we thought it might be an ideal time to take this leadership topic to a national level. But where? Just a few blocks down the street was the National Constitution Center.

CHAPTER 28

What Do We Owe the Women
Who Fought to Secure Our Rights?

I'm a believer in the 3:00 a.m. phenomenon. Some of my best ideas occur in the middle of the night. When they do, I either write them down or give them the survival test. If I can't remember them in the morning, then they probably weren't all that dazzling in the first place. In late 2007, one idea not only passed the test, but it kept me awake the rest of the night. Imagine if we could unite women from all over America to finish the work of the women suffragists in time for the one hundredth anniversary of that landmark in 2020. Imagine . . .

From 2006-2009 I had a tenth-floor office in a building in downtown Philadelphia. It was the last stop for Drexel's Institute for Women's Health and Leadership before moving to a permanent new home on the medical college's campus.

It was a spacious office, with a great view. So great, in fact, that on a clear day you could see all the way to the year 2020.

What was plainly visible was that the centennial of the most significant achievement in the progress of American women was on the near horizon.

I find it fascinating that the best ideas often come about while we're looking for something else. A friend of mine calls it "looking at something and figuring out what else it can be."

That's how real change happens. If others are interested in your original idea, they will quickly make it better by adding several of their own. It only took the first rain to tell the inventors of the automobile that they'd have to come up with windshield wipers, and later someone would figure out how to make them operate at different speeds. The paintbrush was a good idea, followed by the roller and finally, the concept of spray-painting evolved. The garter belt evolved into—yes, pantyhose!

Vision 2020 happened in steps also.

Our dedicated historian at the Institute's Legacy Center recommended that we host a traveling exhibit called "Changing the Face of Medicine: America's Women Physicians," put together by the National Library of Medicine with extensive help from our Archives. After all, over one-half of women physicians in the twentieth century graduated from Woman's Medical College/Medical College of Pennsylvania, one of our predecessor institutions.

The exhibit honors the lives and accomplishments of women who have influenced the practice of medicine. One of the goals is to inspire a new generation of medical pioneers, a goal consistent with the Institute's mission.

It was planned for the fall of 2010 in Philadelphia on the condition that we find a good location for its six-week stay. One of our first considerations was the recently opened National Constitution Center that shared some real estate with Independence Hall and the Liberty Bell in the historic section of Philadelphia. In the summer of 2008, the Constitution Center became the site of then-candidate Barack Obama's defining speech on race relations in America.

But months before that, my 3:00 a.m. idea made its appearance. As worthwhile as the story of women in medicine was, it was just one part of a larger picture of the history of women's leadership. Why not use 2010—just a decade before the one hundredth anniversary of the nineteenth amendment's ratification—to review progress on a wider range of women's issues?

No women were in the room in 1787 when the U.S. Constitution was written, no advocates to remind the nation's founders that "We, the People" ought to be more inclusive than the small print would prove to be.

I've always felt uncomfortable with the idea that in 1920 women *won* the "right" to vote. We always had the "right," but we were never allowed to exercise it because most women were powerless to go up against the male claim of "we know best."

When we visited the Constitution Center to discuss the traveling exhibit, I had a larger agenda in mind and one of the people at the meeting was quick to pick up on the idea of an event with a wider appeal.

The executive in charge of national programs as that time was Jane Eisner, former editor of the *Philadelphia Inquirer*, a respected journalist and one of those "connecting" friends I had known over the years. With her I discussed the idea of a larger salute to women achievers and the opportunity to advance women's leadership. It was a concept to bring together delegates from all fifty states, not only to honor yesteryear, but to put time and energy toward charting what's needed to achieve the suffragists' goal of women's equality. This illustrious group would also develop a plan for the ten years between 2010 and the year 2020.

Happily, the Constitution Center came aboard as a partner with our Institute for Women's Health and Leadership. So along with our idea, we now had a prestigious, almost iconic site. We then came up with a name that captured the centennial celebration as well as our ambitious agenda.

Vision 2020. To which we later added the tag line "Equality in Sight."

The reason a high visibility venue was so important was that we wanted to begin the decade with an action assembly of women leaders. We would use our already-proven "Conversations" format, the lively question-and-answer, no-speeches, approach to communications.

Once conceived, the plan developed rapidly. Eight topics would be explored with an eye toward progress made since the suffragists ran a victory lap in 1920, and the other eye on launching a new momentum toward equality.

We would call the October, 2010, gathering "An American Conversation about Women and Leadership."

On the agenda:

- Politics and Government
- Business, Law, and Finance
- Education
- Engineering, Science and Technology
- Health
- Communications and Media
- Philanthropy, Faith, and Volunteerism
- Arts and Culture

What were our expectations? That bright minds from all fifty states and the District of Columbia would make our two days together an incubator for ideas—one that would mobilize the American conscience to pursue the democratic ideal of gender equality. And that this group of leaders would demonstrate the unity of purpose in our time that the suffragists had demonstrated a century earlier.

I realized, sometime after I had plunged into the excitement of the possibilities of Vision 2020, that I was actually exercising some of the principles that had guided my own life. I was now harvesting what I had worked so long to build into my lifestyle—service to others, coalition building, fundraising, confidence, know-how, and absolute faith in a positive outcome.

Service to others—as I pictured the potential influence of a nationwide surge to improve the lives of women, I could almost hear the words of my father and mother urging me to "live a life from which others benefit because you were there to help."

Coalition building—I envisioned a mammoth coalition transcending geography, race, ethnicity, religion, age, sexual orientation, and political persuasion. It would be the largest tent I would ever put up and would only be as sturdy as the cooperative commitment of the women who stood under it with me.

Fundraising—I felt optimistic enough about our "American Conversation" to book an entire hotel near the National Constitution Center. Knowing that a great deal of money would be needed for Vision 2020 over ten years, I went to meet with Drexel University College of Medicine Dean Richard Homan and Drexel University President Constantine Papadakis. When I told them what I needed—an upfront leap-of-faith contribution of $25,000—I will never forget their instant response. It was yes!

Confidence—There was never any reason for doubt about what we could accomplish. All I needed to do was inventory my lifetime of experiences watching women do remarkable things to overcome barriers, shatter glass ceilings, stand up for their rights, work together for change. We just needed more women to get the message and get engaged.

Know-how—The enormous dimensions of this idea created butterflies, but not fright. I have had both the sense and good fortune to surround myself with talented people who are skilled at putting all the pieces together. There were unknowns, but I believe that stretching is a way you find out how far you can reach.

A positive outcome—Our delegates would be decision-making women, chosen because they refuse to leave other women behind. With those credentials I never harbored a doubt about sending them back to their states to implement a Vision 2020 plan of action.

Before the first delegate was chosen, I imagined the final thought I would impart to the national leaders when the "American Conversation" ended. I would say, "We are saving a seat for you in this hall for 'A Centennial Conversation' in the Year 2020."

The language of the nineteenth Amendment to the U.S. Constitution is not terribly creative. It reads, "The right of citizens of the United States to vote shall not be denied or abridged by the United States or by any state on account of sex."

Despite its simplicity, it took seventy-two years from the Seneca Falls convention in 1848, and a long and complex political and social battle, to have it ratified by the necessary number of states in 1920.

Why August 26 doesn't get more attention I do not understand!

It is the closest to an Independence Day that women have. It was on that date in 1920 when it was certified that the Tennessee Legislature had ratified the nineteenth Amendment. The deciding vote was cast by a young man whose mother told him to "do the right thing."

But when August 26 rolls around each year, it's just another day in a long, hot summer. No fireworks. No parades. No picnics in the park. No marching bands. No chorus of one hundred women standing on the Capitol steps belting out a few verses of "I Am Woman."

Women, proud of our progress, aware of our possibilities, have earned a place at the table of tomorrow. Vision 2020 has a chair for all of us.

In the first stages we needed people to get excited about the idea. Everywhere I went, unsuspecting friends and strangers were subjected to my unrestrained lobbying about the power potential of Vision 2020. I even wooed one of my favorite risk takers, Cathy Ormerod, away from a perfectly good job to become our project director.

Because this was a national program we wanted our board of advisors to be recognized shapers of opinion.

The first asked, Anna Quindlen and Cokie Roberts, agreed to sign on immediately. Anna's writing always resonated with me. One of the special needs of women is self-esteem, and it is difficult to find a better description than Anna's, written back in 1988:

> I read and walked for miles at night along the beach . . . searching endlessly for someone wonderful who would step out of the darkness and change my life. It never crossed my mind that that person could be me.

I had also been a longtime fan of Cokie Roberts and her cool ability to use her reporting skills to get news out of cautious politicians. I loved the dedication note in her book, *Ladies of Liberty*, which included the words: "to my sisterhood, my wonderful women friends . . ." Her comment in the book that "history looks very different through the eyes of women" said so well why Vision 2020 is necessary. Coincidentally, Cokie's father, Hale Boggs, a congressman from Louisiana, had served with and been a friend of my father.

We completed our advisory board with leaders who were doctors, lawyers, educators, athletes, philanthropists, business leaders.

The first major dividends became obvious in October of 2009, exactly one year before our scheduled conversation with women from all fifty states. We invited one hundred of the best and brightest women in the Philadelphia area to another of our BYOB events (Bring Your Own Brain) and well over one hundred attended. We wanted them to come up with cutting edge questions for the 2010 event. They did that . . . and more.

CHAPTER **29**

Can We Change the World by Supporting Each Other?

There are some people I can't even imagine my life without. These are treasured human beings who by example or loyalty or chemistry or sheer talent have helped shape my attitude, bolstered my courage, and tolerated my missteps. They are called friends. They have earned that title by the energy with which they rallied to help me when I was doing good things, and by the equal vigor with which they let me know when I was doing something dumb. Throughout it all, they stood by me. True friendship is seldom tranquil.

Nobody can get there unless everybody gets there.

While that is probably a flawed philosophy, when I express it to women I am trying to convince them that gender equality becomes a more attainable goal if we learn to lead the applause for each other.

This doesn't diminish individual excellence. That's how leaders emerge. What it does, however, is make it possible for all women to know that they can count on other women to help, not hinder, the fulfillment of their dreams.

This coalition of conscience is needed the most when women are under attack and the pressure is on. We have, however, grown up in a counterculture. We've been taught to avoid conflict and controversy and to compete with each other for men's attention—and too often we just aren't there for each other when the going gets tough.

When a story about someone we know appears in the newspaper, and we're certain it's unfair or untrue, why do we remain silent? Why do we condone gossip instead of confronting it?

There are some who will contest my point, who will say gossip is a sport of choice that adds adrenaline to life and can be played in all kinds of weather. And it's harmless.

Except when it isn't.

There's a powerful passage in Kathryn Stockett's 2009 novel *The Help* about the weapons women use against each other which she describes as "a shiny little set of tools, sharp as witches' fingernails, tidy and laid out neat, like the picks on a dentist's tray." I couldn't express better my feelings about vicious, behind-the-back verbal attacks and the failure of some to stop them.

When my daughter's wedding reception was held at the club where my husband plays golf, my political opponents jumped into the press and onto the radio saying the club had no African American members. The reports implied that the club must have a discriminatory admission policy—it didn't—leading to the conclusion we must be racists. They actually threatened to picket the wedding.

Neither the newspapers nor radio accounts mentioned that my daughter was marrying a Latino—some of his family traveled from Argentina and some didn't speak English. Nor did they talk about the two decades I had just spent in fundraising and advocacy for women's causes benefitting African American and other disadvantaged minority women.

What bothered me most were not the cheap charges, but the fact that the people who knew better did not step forward to challenge what was being printed and spoken. I even had a last minute plea from my friend, Senator Harris Wofford, who called from the floor of the U.S. Senate urging me to change the reception's venue. (I didn't.)

In the pursuit of better lives for women, I have experienced the uncomfortable loneliness of being out on a limb while being unfairly attacked by an adversary, with no one coming to my public defense. One of my friends did send me a note after a negative front-page news story. It said, "It's okay to be out on a limb because that's where the fruit is."

I have dealt with the heat because I believed in what I was doing. However, I cannot cope well with the feeling of abandonment by people whom I know feel the way I do about a particular issue or incident.

We need to understand what "together" can do.

A friend of mine told me that she writes at least five letters to the editor every day—in her head. That may help her regulate her own output of steam, but it doesn't do anything for the person or situation that's been publicly misrepresented.

To make a difference, letters to the editor have to be sent.

A century ago Emma Goldman was a prolific activist. That she had communist sympathies earned her a notorious reputation, enough so that she was deported from the United States in the early 1920s to the Soviet Union (she had been born fifty years earlier in Lithuania).

In 1916, when she was still in the United States, authorities arrested her for handing out brochures about contraception, an offense for which she was convicted and incarcerated. She had been in jail before and would be again on far more inflammatory charges, but she felt that merely being in favor of birth control should not be a crime.

What disturbed Emma Goldman even more is that others who shared her view on the issue did not rally to her side. Eventually she would become a mentor to Margaret Sanger, who established Planned Parenthood with principles rooted in Goldman's beliefs about contraception.

In the 1920s, Dr. Emily Mudd, whom I got to know later in her life, used a different strategy to keep a Planned Parenthood clinic open in Philadelphia during this same time period. She stood in the doorway while she was pregnant, and a law prohibiting the arrest of a pregnant woman prevented the police from closing the clinic.

Especially on issues where the outcome has a profound effect on their lives, women need to stand together. "Standing together" does not mean that we are lock-stepped in agreement on every detail of every issue.

That agree/disagree brand of unity was so evident in the preview brainstorming session for Vision 2020. We had assembled 120 women and a "few good men" from the region to help us develop the agenda for the 2010 nationwide "American Conversation about Women and Leadership."

I watched as these energetic leaders formed teams, each group considering one of the topics on the agenda. Their task was to come up with a half-dozen substantive questions in each area—questions that would provoke some heavy thinking toward the goal of advancing women's equality and leadership.

I had the best job that day. I was hosting the sessions, so I was able to listen in on all the groups. It was part of what I had been working to see for the past three plus decades—smart women, and their male allies, seriously engaged in change-making discussions. Sometimes persuasive. Sometimes emotional. Sometimes angry.

And that's okay. Anger without insult is helpful. In my definition of unity, I don't insist that everyone feels exactly the same about an issue. To me, unity for women is being engaged in decision making.

I've observed through the years that women have gradually become more sensitized about our place in society. Many of us have begun to understand that we must support each other, and to think differently about each other.

To get a genuine appreciation of what's possible in her life, a woman must sample its better things. I contend that high on the roster of better things is the discovery that encouraging each other is an enormously satisfying endeavor.

It's not threatening. It's not damaging. It's not fattening.

Over the years I've spent a lot of time "connecting." In fact, Leadership Philadelphia named me as one of the top Connectors in the region in 2008, and it's a title of which I'm proud. In large part, I connect women who are young, looking for a job, new to the area or otherwise in need of information and referrals to people and resources that can help them solve a problem or move ahead. I find this rewarding, and all it takes is some of my time. My husband Paul has often said that I should turn the skill and interest into a business. But the benefit to me is the knowledge that another woman may have an easier time because of my help.

Women are relative newcomers in matters of leadership, at least in significant numbers. I want to see more women in the CEO chair, not because they will bring greatness to the human race, but because they will bring value to the enterprise by unleashing the greatness that is already there.

At the risk of alienating my male friends, the paragraphs just ahead are going to focus on four areas where I feel women have a distinct leadership edge over men.

Women's Leadership Edge No. 1: *Women are more persuasive and effective at molding consensus.*

The stereotype cartoon of four women squabbling about how to divide a lunch check is obsolete. What was portrayed as petty indecisiveness was actually consensus at work—peacefully, fairly, accurately. Women are good at that.

Some years ago I helped form the Rosemary Lane Group, ten women who felt that radio talk shows were dominated by men whose issues and opinions were contrary to our values. We created our own show called *The Way We Hear It*, and I spent thirteen weeks cohosting a two-woman live radio talk show. Unfortunately, we had an unenviable Saturday afternoon time slot and the show didn't survive.

What *did* survive was a positive feeling because we tried. The Rosemary Lane Group considered for a time pooling our own personal financial and managerial resources to buy a station or to try and put the show on some kind of state-wide hookup.

Although we made the decision not to go forward in the end, what impressed me was the cooperative spirit of my partners. We openly aired the pros and cons of proposed actions, and when it came time to reach for consensus, the consensus was already there.

In my experience, when the strong leader in the room is a man, other men are quite compliant to whatever choices the leader has made. But in a room full of women, the strong woman leader often finds her plan questioned, debated, roasted, and hung out to dry. In the end, however, she has a consensus with credibility.

Women's Leadership Edge No. 2: *Women explore with more compassion the impact of a decision on real human beings.*

It's been said that men in business know how to count money better than women, that they know how to get the product out the door faster, and that they are better prepared to deal with competitors.

I don't concede any of that. When given the chance—not often enough—women have proven themselves in engineering, manufacturing, marketing, financial services. When they are elected to public office, they show every bit as much legislative savvy as men and, in general, they bring a lot more sunshine into how laws get passed.

The edge for the woman leader is in her concern for the "customer." In business, the customer is the one who buys the product. In government, the customer is the one who ends up paying more taxes, or dealing with new regulations, or finding out how new legislation affects her family.

These are what I call "the real people." They have managed a household, held a job, raised a family, and had their share of hard times. Many are women. And when it comes to leadership decisions that shape human lives, it is my view that we are better listeners with a natural inclination to be empathetic.

Women's Leadership Edge No. 3: *Women are more patient than men, and more accustomed to multitasking.*

In decision making, patience can be as valuable as speed—not as dramatic, but more carefully constructed. And the ability to juggle multiple priorities is essential in our high-speed culture.

Most women I know, including me, don't like to parallel-park. We will take the time to drive around the block hoping an easy space opens up. "Waste of time," shout the critics. "Common sense," says the woman who prefers an uneventful parking experience, free of scratched fenders and honking horns. That's patience. In the end we find the right parking space. It is the opposite side of the rush-to-judgment coin. Women know a great deal about patience. We've had two hundred years of experience with it.

In terms of multitasking, women are accustomed to balancing a variety of competing responsibilities. In a book called *The Female Advantage: Women's Ways of Leadership*, the authors describe successful women as handling interruptions better than men do. This ability comes from managing child care, car pools, and household responsibilities along with jobs outside the home.

Women's Leadership Edge No. 4: *Women understand men significantly better than men understand women.*

Gender bias on my part? Probably. Female chauvinism? I hope so.

The phrase "women's intuition" is overworked. I prefer to explain our consistency in making good decisions under pressure by calling it "women's judgment."

So many barriers still block American women from leadership roles and the opportunity to take our rightful place. Not ahead of men, not behind them, but side by side, sharing responsibility and reward.

To accomplish this, we have to identify our obstacles and then make the commitment to dismantle them. Facing up to the truth, we will find that one of the key barriers is right there in the mirror—our own reluctance to encourage and support other women. If we wish to impress the world, first we must impress ourselves.

The next step, working with men, is perhaps the most solvable part of a woman's puzzle. It is a bridge waiting to be crossed, for although we are women and men by chance, we are sisters and brothers by choice. We must work together for a more just and humane society.

There exists no good reason to settle for less.

CHAPTER **30**

Is It Age or Conscience That Reminds Us to Mark the Trail Clearly So Others May Follow?

One of the dividends or consequences of achieving even garden variety prominence was that people began to ask me all kinds of questions I hadn't gotten before I became a candidate for political office. It was strange to be asked these questions. What's even stranger was that I started answering them.

While dying holds no appeal for me, I don't worry about it either. Some people fear it. Some even practice dying. I've accepted the reality that I probably won't get everything done that I want to, and that I won't be able to hang around long enough to see how it all comes out. Death is such an unpredictable intruder, taking my brother's best years away from him while extending the lives of my parents beyond the time they would have wanted.

When I was younger, I was preoccupied about when and how I would die because of the tragic and untimely deaths in my family. In my generation on my father's side, there were six girls and three boys. Each of the boys was killed in separate automobile accidents over several decades, my cousins when they were teenagers, my brother at age forty-three.

These days I'm not making any special preparations for when life ends. Occasionally I think about William Holden's line in the movie "*Network*," where he confronts the reality that he's past middle age and says that he knows "the end is closer than the beginning." When I think of that it reminds me of two things.

One is that I really should clean out the attic. I probably won't. Everything in there seems to have made its peace with being ignored. What right after all these years do I have to introduce neatness and precision to a refuge that has so uncomplainingly sheltered stuff I just couldn't throw away? Though I do wonder if that's where my missing shoe is.

The other thought I have is how insistent I am on paying bills promptly. I've never been able to be content with an unpaid invoice. I want my accounts payable out-basket to be empty.

In the larger scope of doing an audit on life, I find myself asking two questions about my balance sheet. They are questions that can properly be put to women of my generation about our contributions to the progress of sisterhood.

What is the balance between what we owe ourselves and what we owe others?

What is the balance between what we owe yesterday and what we owe tomorrow?

Our debt to women heroes of another time—who they were and what they did—is gratitude and respect. They were brave enough, smart enough, independent enough, persistent enough, honorable enough, and caring enough not to postpone freedom for women by delegating to a later generation.

That debt can probably never be marked "paid-in-full," but I feel the slogan, "We've come a long way, baby" has been validated by the positive progress of the past half-century. Our most useful gift to the future, to those young twenty-first century women who will pick up the baton, would be to provide some advice and instruction on how to prepare for running their leg of the relay.

I liken it to packing for a trip to equality.

Equality can be found on the map somewhere on the other side of waters only partially crossed, with mountains still to be scaled. Women making the trip will want to use carry-on luggage that fits conveniently in the overhead compartment of life. The items you need to pack are things you never want to be far away from. And do not check your luggage or it could get lost along the way. Once misplaced, the will to rediscover your resolve is hard to trace.

By the time I became an adult I knew something about language, math, literature, and music. What I didn't know was the other lessons life would require. I didn't know how to pack my carry-on bag. I think I do now. I suggest a dozen items.

1. Be sure to include a lifetime supply of *courage*. Whether you are traveling alone or, hopefully, with a coalition of women and men

with shared values, you will need to withstand the criticism of those who try to intimidate you into cancelling the trip. At the very least they will second-guess you along the way. Courage is a habit which gets stronger the more you use it. Use it often enough and it becomes a normal part of your lifestyle. Don't leave home without it.

2. Pack plenty of *communication skills*. From the moment you decide to be a leader in advancing the progress of women, or an example, or both, you are in sales. You will be trying to sell something the world does not yet have—equality for women. All of this sales work will flourish if you can write coherently, speak fluently and think creatively. Remember too, to consider your audience, because you cannot succeed until they read, hear and understand what you've said and take action on it.

3. Bring along the best brand of *integrity* you can find. It's one item they can never take away from you. Women have had to overcome indignities and disrespect for so long that we ought to remember not to get caught up in the same trap. You may be the smartest woman in town, but knowledge without integrity is an empty vessel.

4. You'll need *binoculars*. Not just any binoculars, but those specially equipped to see around the next generation. Without visionaries, civilization stands still and progress stalls. Unless women leaders continue to push the envelope of change, that envelope will be sealed, and the girls now growing into women will have to settle for the partial progress we've achieved. If you think everything is just fine for women right now, you can leave the binoculars behind.

5. Package a *sense of humor* for the trip. One of the most effective ways to approach a serious issue like women's search for safety, or economic security, is to not take yourself too seriously. To avoid anxiety you need regular doses of laughter. The information that kindergarten pupils laugh three hundred times a day and adults laugh fifteen times a day jolts me. What happens to us in between?

6. You'll need some *glue*, preferably industrial-strength, to keep your perseverance together. For an adequately motivated woman, rejection is just a pause that calls for redrafting the strategy. This

is a particularly opportune area for women to help each other. In explaining her own perseverance, Susan B. Anthony said, "Failure is impossible." For me, the tougher the battle, the more glorious the victory. Make that a large tube of glue.

7. Bring your *work ethic*. You may want to pack this where you can get to it easily. You'll need it a lot. Women understand hard work, and when we put our minds to it, no one can outwork us. That's a decision we make.

8. Don't forget to carry some *cash*. A woman who has a bank account of her own has already defined independence. I cannot forget my father driving through a snowstorm to deliver $250 to me—he left it at the reception desk on my wedding night!—so I would have money of my own on my honeymoon. He guessed correctly that I was not thinking about the possibility of needing my own money as a newlywed. Cash and other assets will help your trip.

9. Bring all the *time* you can squeeze into the bag. Better yet, bring a knack for managing that time. Time is like the circus, always packing up and leaving town. How we spend our time determines how serious we are about our goals and those lost hours are never coming back. You are the sole owner of your time. Treat every minute like you'll never see it again, because you won't.

10. You'll need *optimism*. Every dream I've chased has been accompanied by my unshakeable optimism about the outcome. Going into any endeavor with a belief that you're going to fail practically guarantees that result. I recognize that an optimist is wrong as often as a pessimist, but she's much happier! She believes the best is yet to come, and believing is where leadership begins.

11. Before you zip the bag, be sure to remember *generosity*. We are more fulfilled when we share our time, talent, and treasure; and it's important also to be generous with your praise of people who share in your success. Generosity of spirit creates an atmosphere that will virtually guarantee the recipient's enthusiasm and loyalty the next time you come to call with an idea that can't possibly work, but does.

12. Final item: fold in another *empty bag*. You'll need it when you get to where you're going and decide, as all women leaders do, to go a little further. That's when you'll need additional items like momentum, humility, desire, goals, imagination, power—and a heart with which to embrace them.

Depositing a legacy of advice with women who are eager to continue what others started is a fairly straightforward exercise. All I've had to do is live long enough to experience challenges many women encounter, absorb the turbulence that came my way, and imagine clearly what a better America this will be when we stop trumping our partner's ace.

Let's start with a fresh deck.

CHAPTER 31

Have You Ever Seen a Hearse with a Luggage Rack?

I like to think positive thoughts. Like imagining older women living out their lives with purpose, dignity, and economic security. Or teenage girls having respect for themselves and each other and being treated as equals by their male peers. Or perhaps all women being able to have healthy and fulfilling careers. Will the women who today control a large percentage of philanthropic dollars identify with these same possibilities?

When foundations or wealthy individuals proudly point to how brilliantly they have managed their funds, reduced their risks or played it safe with their grant money, I'm tempted to remind them not only that "you can't take it with you," but also "you can't send it on ahead."

I tend to measure charity in terms that probably won't get me invited onto a foundation's board or appointed as a financial advisor for wealth management.

Don't tell me what's on your balance sheet. Tell me what's in your heart.

Don't show me your financial return on investment. Show me another ROI—return on innovation. How many lives have you improved this year?

Forget your state-of-the-art system for screening out proposals. Tell me instead about your "screening in" intuition.

I find it thrilling that so much of the philanthropic wealth of America is in the hands of women. I expect to be even more elated when a larger chunk of that money is directed to changing women's second-class status and addressing the needs of those who have been systematically sidelined by society.

When I was growing up, the subject of money was off-limits, and the message was that it was impolite to discuss financial matters. That rule applied especially to women.

It was okay for my father to remind us frequently how poor he had been as a youngster and while in college, where he told us of repairing holes in his trousers by cutting up his hat to make patches and walking on the opposite side of the street when passing the drugstore because he didn't have a nickel to spend. The moral of his stories was that we should appreciate what we had and be frugal in every way. My father also had some advice for me when I became a married adult—he insisted that I keep my own checking account and keep my money separate from Paul's.

What I came to realize in my thirties was that my situation was pretty much unique among my peers. Most of my friends were homemakers/volunteers—as I was during that decade—but I noticed that none had her own checking account. Instead, they had to negotiate with their husbands for spending money or "allowances" and had very little decision-making authority over expenditures beyond basic household needs.

In the seventies, I recall how some were trapped in bad marriages and several had their marriages end in messy divorces. Those women found themselves in radically changed financial circumstances, with little or no income. In one case, the wife took the furniture, wedding gifts, and everything she could manage and left the house while her husband was at work. He had shut down her access to their joint checking account and she was desperate.

My parents' careful management of funds, my father's success in business and public service, and their parental authority over me during some turbulent growing-up years, coupled with my on-and-off earned income, resulted in my economic independence as an adult woman. I would never be trapped in an unhappy relationship or constrained in my decision making about my values and priorities.

It was financial independence that enabled me to run for political office and that has given me the opportunity to make charitable gifts. Both have been liberating experiences. I wish all women had the freedom to make those choices.

I wish also that we would learn to give in proportion to our ability, but I have observed that many women who have the means are reluctant to make large donations. For a variety of reasons, women tend to make small gifts, whether to our colleges—many of which have faltered as a result—or to other causes we care about.

I have believed for a long time that if women used our economic power—whether through giving, investing or purchasing—to advance our views and values, American society would change for the better. We could elect political candidates who represent our priorities. We could influence commercial sponsors to think twice before bankrolling offensive TV shows. We could provide more and better services and advocacy for women and children who are abused, neglected, or disadvantaged in other ways.

What will it take to awaken women to the power we have?

We make most of the health care decisions. We are by far the majority of consumers of goods and services. We are now the largest proportion of the workforce—for the first time outnumbering employed men. And we are the frontline influences on the next generation. Can't we find the time to get organized and focus on creating the kind of world we want our children and grandchildren to live in?

Is there a way we could allocate a percentage of the charitable dollars controlled by women and create a massive central fund aimed at solving problems that, traditionally, have been treated in a piecemeal fashion? It would have to be big. As mentioned earlier, "big" is not automatically bad. I believe in "big." It takes a big government, big business, big educations to solve the big problems. "Big" takes a beating in political speeches, but I don't believe the speakers really mean it.

As important as the corner grocery is, it can't handle the food distribution load of the supermarkets supplying food for a population of 300 million.

As nostalgic as we get about the country doctor making house calls, "big" healthcare demands spacious, high-tech hospitals with large, versatile staffs.

Artists and poets make a living glorifying the beauty of lonely paths carved out of a forest, but America moves on superhighways built with "big" government support.

It therefore follows that if significant changes are to be made to correct past inequities and offer the opportunities women have been denied for two centuries, big dollars will be needed to change entrenched attitudes, institutions and policies.

A National Clearinghouse for Women's Equality is what I envision, and it would be different from anything that currently exists.

Different because it would bring together the many national organizations working on behalf of women and girls and create a heightened focus on specific barriers that are common to the majority of women. It would pinpoint actions to be taken, mobilize the human resources to achieve solutions, and draw on the necessary funding from the unified pool of dollars contributed by individuals and institutions.

The Clearinghouse would set very public goals and timetables for the correction of each problem—whether it's the portrayal of women and girls in the media, the way women are targeted for violence, or how we continue to be underrepresented in government.

The National Clearinghouse for Women's Equality would advocate responsibilities with the same emphasis it would bring to women's rights. Those include a woman's responsibilities to herself, her family, her country—and to other women.

There's a reason for selecting the term "clearinghouse." We are overdue to start "clearing" away the obstacles that have blocked women's path to full participation in shaping our nation's course since the Pilgrims first rushed to America to escape—of all things—oppression.

There is a lot of "clearing" to be done. Attitudes. Disrespect. Unequal pay. Harassment. Job denial. Physical and emotional violence. Neglected health care.

And there is a need to exchange information, align strategies and work together to achieve big goals. In the early 1980s I helped found a national coalition of women's funds which was initially called the National Network of Women's Funds, and is now known as the Women's Funding Network (WFN).

There were five women's funds in the U. S. at that time—foundations and federations, of which Women's Way was one—when we met in San Francisco to form the original national network. Today, the WFN has grown into an international organization with over 130 member funds. Those organizations mostly support local or regional programs for women, although the Ms. Foundation has grantees across the United States. Either the WFN or the newer Women Donors Network (WDN) could take the lead in uniting our financial clout nationally.

We need to think strategically about how to lead, to serve, to give, and to achieve together.

Ten years from now, the National Clearinghouse for Women's Equality could celebrate the centennial of women's suffrage with a program report and action agenda for the rest of the twenty-first century. This would be a great way to say thank–you to the generations who lit the candle by demonstrating how much brighter we can make it burn.

Why do I think of Louise deKoven Bowen? Probably because she devoted her adult life, her wealth, and her fund-raising skills to social welfare action.

Chicago was her base. Jane Addams and her Woman's Club at Hull House got her started.

For forty years before Addams' death in 1935, and for another nine years, Bowen was the driving force behind Hull House. She became a critical link in the social service network of Chicago, and an effective voice across the nation.

Louise Bowen had access to power and money, and the leadership ability and commitment to create successful outcomes. Through her friend Cyrus McCormick, she won a minimum wage for the women of the International Harvester Company. She lectured nationally for women's suffrage.

Two principles guided her social action. First, she had a determination to hold herself accountable for the manner in which she lived her life. Second, she made a decision to put her own considerable wealth to work while she was still alive.

I don't have the numbers, but if we added up all the potential Louise Bowens there are right now in America, and assembled them in the same stadium, I'm certain that by sundown we would have the National Clearinghouse for Women's Equality I envision.

Going forward, I see a better way to make a difference. We must unite the forces of philanthropy to achieve the big changes that won't happen unless women decide to make them happen.

We've set our sights too low for too long. We've been grateful for crumbs when we should have insisted on whole loaves. We can achieve so much more if we set aside our differences, identify our common concerns and use our substantial resources—time, talent and money—to claim the power we have. If organizations unite, with their millions of members, and philanthropists unite, with their millions of dollars, we can change the world.

CHAPTER 32

How Will We Know When We've Arrived at Our Destination?

When a woman decides to blend her personal agenda with a larger cause—the advancement of *all* women—life somehow begins to make more sense. There is a special worth in rallying a coalition of women behind a cause. Your value system, no matter how good it is, takes a sudden jump to a higher place. One benefit I noticed after making up my mind to help fix what wasn't working for women was that all the other decisions in my life became easier.

"Life is to be lived," said actress Katharine Hepburn. "If you have to support yourself, you had bloody well better find some way that is going to be interesting. And you don't do that by sitting around wondering about yourself."

When Katharine Hepburn spoke, people listened. Especially women. It wasn't just that voice that virtually dared you to drop whatever else you were thinking about and pay attention.

In 2009 I enjoyed the privilege of emceeing at the presentation of the Katharine Hepburn Medal to Jane Golden, who caught the eye of the world with the magnificent Mural Arts Program she created in Philadelphia. Her ability to galvanize inner-city people and inspire art that covers the exteriors of buildings with striking portraits of city life earned her the Hepburn Medal, which is presented by Bryn Mawr College, where the four-time Academy Award winner went to school.

Previously, the award had gone to only two people—actresses Lauren Bacall and Blythe Danner. I looked around the National Constitution Center at all the people who were there that evening. Most of them were women of admirable achievement in their own right. I thought for a moment about the luxury of having this pause in my hurry-up life to appreciate the genuine progress that women have made.

I've been fortunate to grow up with a generation of trailblazers. I came from a family that had strong women on almost every branch of the tree. They fortified me with confidence in my ability to lead and succeed while living a useful life and making things better for those who would follow.

Girls born today have more choices than I had at their age. I don't envy them that—I applaud it. And I've done what I can to help make it possible.

Girls can enter adulthood feeling more sure of themselves now. They can choose the kind of work they do and where they do it. They can work for someone, or they can have a lot of "someones" work for them.

As encouraging as all that opportunity sounds, women's lives are still highly complex and increased choices can bring increased stress. There is much for new generations to do to finish the work of their older sisters.

We can learn a lot from listening to the women I saw that February evening at the Award Program. There is a special value in an alliance of women with a purpose. Sometimes that value is unspoken, while at other times it is shouted loud enough to be heard by the next generation.

Women who have lived through the dramatic transitions of the past decades—from being taken for granted to being taken seriously—understand that with age and experience comes strength. They know that alliances *do* matter. Most women of my generation are good at being inclusive because we know what being excluded is like. We are good at identifying what first-class citizenship is because we've experienced what second-class treatment does to a woman's confidence and self-esteem.

I believe that everything up to now has been a first draft.

That means that every sexist comment a woman has endured, every put-down encountered, every underpaid job survived—we can chalk it all up to preparation for the beginning of something new, something better.

When Women's Way in Philadelphia reached its twenty-five-year anniversary, I was invited to come back and help stage a celebration for the fundraising organization I had proudly had a hand in founding and guiding through its early years.

I had a few precious moments at the podium at the beautiful new Kimmel Center for the Performing Arts on a night of highlights that included Lily Tomlin and so many memorable moments. I looked out at the full house of 2,500 enthusiastic women (and some men), and I thought about how far we had come from those first shaky days back in the '70s when we wondered if women really could emerge from their individual isolation and pool their resources for a common purpose.

I resisted letting my remarks focus on the past. I've always advised people not to look back unless that's the direction they intend to go. Nor do I overplay the distant future. I am content with Maya Angelou's assessment that "the future is plump with promise."

Except for the inspiration I get from history and my daydreams about a time not yet here, I tend to dwell very little on either extreme. I have an absolutely absorbing affair going on with the here and now.

Today is my Tinker Toy set. It's where I can begin to connect the sticks and spools that will help me to shape what tomorrow is really going to look like. Legos have pretty much replaced Tinker Toys in the modern moment of children who like to permit their imagination to take them where it will, but though toys and technology may change, curiosity about our own competence should not.

On that Women's Way night, the program opened with one hundred women and girls on stage singing the Helen Reddy anthem, "I Am Woman." These were not professional singers, but they could carry a tune. They had been in a high school chorus at one time, or were now. The youngest was twelve—she had a solo part. The oldest was eighty-one. They were secretaries, attorneys, teachers, stay-at-home household managers, doctors, and sales clerks.

They were strangers when they assembled to practice for their three minutes in the spotlight. I went to one of their rehearsals, and I could sense immediately that they were motivated by more than the thrill of a brief brush with show business, something to share with friends at work the next day in one of those guess-what-I-did-last-night moments.

As they cautiously went about their limited choreography and put together their voices, you could tell that they understood the power of unity. They knew that the message of Helen Reddy's song went well beyond the lyrics. They saw that their hundred voices could take her message and expand it sufficiently to encourage people to live it as well as to listen to it.

Near the end of the evening's program, just before the traditional "Pomp and Circumstance" video, we announced the winner of a poll we had taken earlier among the audience members.

The question we asked was: "Who will be the first woman on Mt. Rushmore?"

Rosa Parks got a lot of votes. So did Hillary Clinton. And Sacagawea. And Amelia Earhart. The clear winner, however, was Eleanor Roosevelt.

It was an undisputed election. No calls for a recount. No hanging chads. The ballot-counting committee was headed by my friend Stephanie Naidoff, who, more than incidentally, had been largely responsible for raising much of the money and managing the construction of the Kimmel Center for the Performing Arts itself.

Backstage, just before Stephanie went out to announce the crowd's choice for the next Mt. Rushmore carving, she was asked if the vote was close. Stephanie's typically generous smile was at its best when she said, "It was a landslide."

I asked myself why this audience, many of them in their twenties and thirties, would select a woman who had been dead for forty years. Though it initially puzzled me, I felt good that they were placing value on women who had proven to be extraordinary pioneers of change.

Two Eleanor Roosevelt sayings have challenged me throughout my adult life, one of them so powerful it has found a prominent place on the wall of whatever office I happened to be occupying. It says, "The future belongs to those who believe in the beauty of their dreams."

The companion line is "You must do the thing you think you cannot do." These words helped me to dig out of the frequent avalanches of adversity in which I was submerged.

In an all-girls' school, playing the male lead in *Pirates of Penzance*. *You must do the thing you think you cannot do.*

In New York, refusing secretarial jobs to hold out for the advertising opening that got my career started. *You must do the thing you think you cannot do.*

In a high-profile U.S. Senate race with the odds stacked against me. *You must do the thing you think you cannot do.*

Confronting the United Way in a desperate battle to raise funds for women's causes; challenging the status quo in a well-known club with discriminatory policies; energizing federal employees in a regional office of the U.S. Department of Health and Human Services; finding a place in academia to continue furthering women's leadership; creating a revolutionary concept, Vision 2020, to mobilize women nationwide for a major leap forward in the pursuit of gender equality. *You must do the thing you think you cannot do.*

As proud as I am of today's women, I would still ask that they read the rest of the memo. That's the part that says our commitment to each other is very much like a piano. It needs regular tuning.

I still hear the majority of women say they don't want anything to do with politics. That it's too messy and controversial.

That's the argument women have been using for years—while at the same time complaining about taxes they think are too high, schools they regard as inadequate, laws they see as unfair, and candidates they believe are untrustworthy.

What in the world is so important on the first Tuesday after the first Monday in November that we can't find the time to vote? What is it that prevents us from pitching in to work for a candidate or, better yet, to be one?

I recently heard about a study of women's voting which showed that many women don't vote because of a lack of confidence. Confidence in their knowledge? Confidence in their choices? Confidence in themselves?

We should be savvy enough to know that the politicians who vote against things that are important to women are sent to office not by our foes who vote, but by our friends who don't!

Participation, speaking out, putting your name on the line—these are the requirements for twenty-first century women who understand that we must pay now for the possibilities, or we will pay later for the consequences.

There is too much still to be accomplished for women to declare victory and to leave the rest of the unfinished agenda to "someone else."

We should know by now who the "someone else" is. It is us.

Harriet Beecher Stowe began her writing career in hopes of supplementing her husband's modest salary as a faculty member at Bowdoin College in Maine. Of all her writings—her essays, articles, short stories, novels—the words I most vividly recall were about perseverance.

She said, "When you get in a tight place and everything goes against you till it seems as though you could not hold on a minute longer, never give up then, for that is just the time and the place the tide will turn."

The tide is turning favorably for women a little every day, and it will continue to flow our way if we have the good judgment to emulate our heroes who never stopped believing. Now, we are in need of a fresh supply of heroes.

Sometimes an overnight success takes a century or two.

CHAPTER 33

Will the Wind Be in Our Face, or at Our Back?

Sometimes I wonder if I'll know when I should stop working. When will my energy and interest in making the world a better place for women begin to wane? Will I know when it is time for me to become a spectator? Of one thing I'm certain—that time has clearly not yet arrived.

During the vigorous presidential campaign of 2008—first the Democratic primary battle between Hillary Clinton and Barack Obama, then the contest between Obama and John McCain, I visited the elementary school where my granddaughter was also running for office in a school election.

Mae was nine years old at the time. She was running for president of the fourth grade.

By then I was already emotionally and practically into my Vision 2020 initiative, a tribute to the upcoming centennial of the suffrage amendment ratified in 1920, and a focal point for rallying women throughout America to finish the equality goals that others had begun.

As I encouraged my nine-year-old granddaughter in her campaign, I came to a realization. She will be twenty-one when the Year 2020 rolls around. If we can achieve the changes that permit women, once and for all, to stand as equals with men, the world that Mae and her younger cousin Chloe will inhabit will be a dramatically improved one.

What my view of those young girls told me was that there can be no letup for those of us who feel the obligation to continue to equalize opportunities, amend policies, influence attitudes, eliminate stereotypes, and resist discrimination.

Today's young women find an array of choices that are much more in focus than I ever knew—choices not just for personal growth, but for the chance to make contributions to the national good.

It's been clear to me for a long time that I enjoy setting ambitious goals. I love to take on challenges, particularly if they involve changing a status quo that I view as wrong, unjust, or complacent. And I've been able to transfer my enjoyment of being a "change agent" to other women, persuading them to join me in my endeavors.

Rosemarie Greco, a woman of superb achievement in business and public service and my co-chair for Vision 2020, wrote a treasured note to me shortly after I had the privilege of speaking about her generosity and leadership in the early nineties. It was at the Multiple Sclerosis Hope Award Dinner in Philadelphia, where Rosemarie was being honored, as she has been so often, for her work with others.

When her note came to me, I read it twice that day and have thought of its message many times since.

She said, "I liken you to a torch of light. Some people are afraid of torches. After all, they do not fit into a box. They must not be contained. They are fueled by their environment. Most other people, however, are mesmerized by the hope torches spread."

I was flattered and deeply touched by her eloquence, and I was pleased far beyond the praise for me by the very fact that she had sent the note. Not surprisingly, Rosemarie truly understands the value of women supporting, encouraging, and inspiring each other.

I have been asked more than a few times how I define "a useful and honorable life," a phrase used to describe my father in an editorial following his death. I don't have a specific definition. I wish I did. I'm not aware of any magical blueprint, but if pressed on the subject, I would encourage young people to think of life in four segments.

In the first twenty years, get excited about many things and get very good at three or four. It's called "identifying your talent." Your education is about developing your curiosity and enhancing your personality. Sometimes it's tempting to get so busy earning a diploma that we become robots to a system that can chip away at our originality.

In the next twenty years—that time between twenty and forty (some call it evolving from the *Partridge Family* into *Desperate Housewives*)—learn to replace the expectations of others with some of your own. These are the early career years. They are also the reproductive years and they are what I call the "rapid years." If not lived a day at a time, achievement-by-achievement, adventure-by-adventure, they will evaporate at blurring speed.

From forty to sixty, enjoy what you have already built into your life—courage, confidence, commitment. At this point you should have made most of the mistakes you're going to make. Whatever caution you carefully nurtured to avoid risk should be washed away by your conviction that it is finally "your time." It is your time to excel, to lead, to reach out, and to help others.

From sixty on, these are the "power" years. This is when you have the assembled lessons of your life. You have causes you believe in—and you shouldn't care if someone is critical of them. It's the time of life when you discover you are really the same person you were as a child. The only change can be found in the deterioration of the mirrors in your house. This child you liked so well now shows up in the mirror with a different face and body. Time to write a letter to the manufacturer.

Happily, though, by this time we don't care as much about our appearances and have become more interested in our thoughts, deeds, and experiences. I've noticed that when women decide to fulfill all the potential we have by using our wonderful brainpower instead of warehousing it, and when we insist on full citizenship, society doesn't quite know what to do about us.

That's when the GNG goes up. That's the Gross National Guilt. This guilt involves postponing issues by deliberately *not* making decisions that need to be made. In parliamentary procedure it's called "tabling" the matter, an action that is usually followed by a changing of the subject or calling for a committee to do a study.

Whatever that "table" is, women must be determined to tip it over.

I commend to today's women a series of actions that probably won't get done unless we take the leadership to see that they happen.

I commend . . .

To your attention, the challenge of improving the health and well-being of women and families who are economically disadvantaged and medically underserved.

To your conscience, the education and training of males and females of all ages in skills and attitudes that will make them competitive in the marketplace and respectful of each other.

To your sense of priorities, the need in this land of abundance for every person to have a dependable supply of nourishing food and shelter.

To your fundamental fairness, the correction of abuses against women—unequal pay, workplace harassment, physical and emotional assault.

To your mathematical logic, the reversal of the overwhelming gender imbalance related to positions of power in government, in business, in science, in media, and in communications.

That should be enough to get us started!

Do you wonder, as I do, if these inequities would not already have been corrected if the U.S. Senate had fifty-two women and forty-eight men; if the U.S. House had 236 women and 199 men—as proper proportioning of the elected government would provide?

Isn't it reasonable to believe that if the corrective actions needed to bring about equality between the sexes have not been taken in over two hundred years, they are not likely to happen under the male-dominated power structure that has perpetuated the one-sided society in which we live?

As we pursue our goal of equality, let's not set traps for ourselves. Let's avoid envy and criticism of each other. Revolutions, particularly peaceful ones, don't go well if we waste our energy with women battling other women over the small issues. When that happens, we become too content with half victories. We settle for the satisfaction of achievements to date and decide to play defense by building a moat around a castle that is still under construction.

If we are willing to rewrite rules of conduct crafted without our input, I believe we should be able to give up standing on any real or imagined pedestals of the past, and start standing on some principles of progress.

Candy Lightner showed us something about women and the power of unity.

On May 3, 1980, her daughter Cari's life was ended by a drunk driver. Candy Lightner, in the midst of stress and sorrow, made a decision that would echo throughout America. Only four days after her daughter's death she sat down with a few friends to see what could be done to call attention to the tragic impact of drunken driving. That's when Mothers Against Drunk Driving (MADD) took its first steps toward becoming the voice of national outrage.

Candy's "few friends" grew to twenty for a demonstration in Sacramento, state capital of California. By the time they went to Washington to march in protest in front of the White House, they numbered just over one hundred.

She and her followers were pleading for someone to listen so the carnage on the highways caused by people who drank irresponsibly could be reduced. The result was that nearly four hundred chapters of MADD have been organized around the world, more than four hundred new laws in all fifty states were written to deal with drunken driving, and a national commission against drunk driving was formed.

Perhaps even more telling was the creation, by young people, of SADD—Students Against Drunk Driving.

The message of Candy Lightner's story is clear—if you care enough about a purpose, about seeing what's wrong and doing something about it—there is no limit to the possibilities.

What a wonderful time it is to be a woman! Every day we are being schooled in the lessons of self-reliance, self-esteem, self-fulfillment. How high we are able to grade our papers will determine how much remains to be done by future generations. Will they be just as determined, devoted, committed as we are?

My nine-year-old granddaughter Mae came up with a slogan for her election campaign—"Vote for Mae. She'll save the day." She also wrote a speech in which she made some comments about her great-grandparents, her grandparents, and the 2008 presidential election. She then said, "Okay, enough about that. Now let's talk about the fourth grade!" When I heard that, I knew. She won't wait for her ship to come in—she'll swim out to meet it.

She's on her way.

CHAPTER 34

Can the Thirty-three Previous Chapter Questions Each Be Answered in Fifty Words or Less?

Yes. Here goes . . .

1. As we reach for the peaks, can we cope with the valleys?

    Trying to overturn a culture of control that has been rigid in its rules is an adventure that promises and delivers adversity. To secure our own independence, women must prepare for an emotional roller coaster.

2. How do we measure the impact of "family?"

    Family has been accurately described as a "dear octopus from whose tentacles we never quite escape, nor in our hearts do we ever quite wish to." Through good times and not-so-good, "family" remains a core resource and influence on our lives.

3. If the elevator to independence is out of order, are we willing to take the stairs?

    "Pressure is a privilege," said Billie Jean King, "champions adjust." The greater the challenge, the more satisfying the success. When one door closes, women need the agility to find another.

4. Will justice come if we wait long enough?

    Not a chance. One thing we can count on—equity for women won't be achieved if we retreat into a patient calm. People in power take that as a sign of weakness, a symbol of acceptance, and the status quo will be perpetuated.

5. Are "conforming" and "confining" the same word in a woman's dictionary?

> They are if you conform to rules that unfairly restrict your freedom to live a life free of harassment and discrimination. Obeying the law is essential, but protesting rules that are unjust, especially those that oppress women, is an act of courage and a prerequisite for change.

6. How can we redefine power?

> Acquiring power for the right reasons is an act of love, so it makes sense to study people who know how to use it. Imitate what they do that earns your admiration and be sure to edit out what you want no part of.

7. Whose expectations are they anyway?

> There was a time not so long ago when girls' goals were far more modest than those of boys. It was thought that gender competition might damage male self-esteem and take women out of their assigned roles. That time is filed away in history. It needs to stay there.

8. How is profit measured in a nonprofit world?

> The bottom line for those who are mission-driven is the satisfaction and joy that come from our work to improve people's lives. Helping women discover opportunities and other, more fulfilling, ways to enjoy life brings profit beyond measure.

9. If we can see the power of one, can we imagine the power of many?

> Rosa Parks demonstrated the power of one. The Million Mom March showcased the power of many. Both individuals and coalitions can influence change in a meaningful, sometimes

dramatic, way. Either way, the twin sister of power is responsibility. It comes with the territory.

10. Why is the door to opportunity for women often marked "Push?"

Yesterday has not been kind to women, unless your favorite musical instrument is second fiddle. Why return to the scene of neglect and put-down when just over the horizon awaits a new era called equality?

11. Connections and persistence—is there a better pair of partners?

Getting others to help open doors is a legitimate contact sport. Keeping those doors open, saying, "I'll take it from here," depends on your ability to demonstrate value. When you do that, don't forget to leave an opening for the next woman who knocks.

12. What can we learn from women's history?

Women's history has been inadequately preserved and poorly recorded. As a consequence, there's been a lot of wheel reinvention. We yearn to be inspired, and should be, by the unfinished agenda for women's full equality. Inspiration fuels our energy. We should add our own examples for others to learn from.

13. Are women leaders different from men?

In a workplace, where teamwork dominates the culture, the boss's gender ought not to matter. But a woman's leadership and management style, grounded in the multiple life roles she probably plays, may enhance the collaborative environment.

14. When will we cheer for overdogs?

The origins of women's competition with each other probably go back to the beginning of time. A spirited competitive nature can be healthy, but envy and jealousy have often obstructed our enjoyment of each other's success. It's time to recognize that when one woman moves up, we all win.

15. If women are single-issue candidates, what is the issue?

> The issue is justice. The dictionary refers to it as fairness, impartiality. Justice is the use of power to uphold what is right. When we achieve justice for women, all other issues will follow.

16. Can we handle the loss of privacy in a run for public office?

> This is a harsh political reality. Everything you thought was yours alone becomes fair game. Bank balance, religious faith, family, every cherished aspect of personal life—the press will write about it and your opponents will abuse it.

17. Why is politics so personal?

> Attacks on your character are part of the toll paid to cross the bridge from private citizen to public punching bag. Lacking skeletons in your closet, your adversaries will build a new closet—and stock it.

18. If we spend too much time looking in the rearview mirror, will we miss our turn?

> Regrets don't help attain the goals just ahead. "Would you have done things differently?" is not the question. "*Will* you do things differently from now on?" That's a challenge deserving of your best response.

19. How can we find victory and reject victimhood?

> Women can generally be found in life's pool, swimming among the expectations of parents, children, partners, friends, clients, bosses. What may be missing are expectations of our own, saving part of our life for pure, old-fashioned self-interest.

20. How do we define courage?

> When we refuse to compromise our integrity, even in the face of enormous pressure or temptation, we stand tall as an example to

others. Clarity of values and principles is the starting point, but that's only useful if those standards are expressed and adhered to.

21. Controversy—where would we be without it?

We need to learn to welcome it, not walk away from it. The advances women have made—the attitudes and institutions that have changed—did not occur in a vacuum of reverence for things as they were. If standing for what we believe is controversial, so be it.

22. Can we learn to embrace change that will help us?

When we struggle for so long for small gains, there is a natural tendency to consolidate that progress and not risk losing it for another promise that may be unkept. Breaking out of that shell of caution and trusting change—that is a goal to reach for.

23. In our search for who we are, is it useful to return to where we came from?

It's probably entertaining, but not abundantly productive. Whatever good or bad fortune propelled us to where we are, we remain there only by choice. Dreaming what we want to be, and then doing something about it may be a more exciting use of our gifts, and our options.

24. Why is decision making so difficult, so demanding, so irresistible?

Making decisions is about responsibility, which we love, and results which we can't predict. Responsibility is the prime consequence of the freedom women seek and are gradually achieving. To shy away from making the decisions that go with it is unthinkable.

25. Is truth closer when we ask all the questions, even though we may not like the answers?

Just because we can't choreograph the answers we get is no reason to hold back in asking the tough questions. Postponing the acceptance of the truth, hoping it will change by the time you hear it, only allows one's anxiety to accrue. Truth has a special power.

26. Will we ever act like the majority we are?

If we pause long enough to add up the numbers, we will realize that our 52 percent of the population represents a power waiting to be exercised. A democracy thrives on numbers. Thriving time is here.

27. Dick and Jane. Jack and Jill. Romeo and Juliet. Does first billing matter?

Education has smoothed the path for men to achieve leadership, while women historically have been channeled to supporting roles. In the 21st century, a balanced educational experience will open the opportunity door, but individuals must demonstrate the will to use it.

28. What do we owe the women who fought to secure our rights?

We owe them a demonstration that we have the capability and commitment to work together to finish the work they began. In doing so, we will make it clear, as they did, that we do not seek power over men, but over ourselves.

29. Can we change the world by supporting each other?

Mutual support ought to be our strong suit. If we will widen our lens we will see that when one woman makes a breakthrough, the climate improves for all women. Helping each other is fundamental to our overdue goal of equality.

30. Is it age or conscience that reminds us to mark the trail clearly so others may follow?

Conscience is the correct answer. By now, we should be conscious of our obligation to show other women how we won, and what happened when we didn't. To keep secrets of success to yourself is to stop women's progress where it stands.

31. Have you ever seen a hearse with a luggage rack?

The joy in philanthropy is in giving, not hoarding. Delayed giving may assure you of praise in your obituary, but donations made now enable you to see projects advanced, lives changed. If your cup runneth over, plenty of deserving saucers are nearby.

32. How will we know when we've arrived at our destination?

In the search for "who" and "when" answers about finding our future leaders, we can turn to two reliable questions: If not us, who? If not now, when?

33. Will the wind be in our face, or at our back?

Women have made enormous progress toward equality, and there are many encouraging signs for the future. We must seize the momentum and recognize that justice awaits only our willingness to achieve it. Those who want us to slow down are counting on our complacency. They're guessing wrong.

INDEX

Edwards Brothers,Inc!
Thorofare, NJ 08086
01 October, 2010
BA2010274